Valley Places, Valley Faces

Photography by **Rebecca Rivera**

Text by **Eileen Mattei**

Design by **Vanessa Lively**

A publication of the
Rio Grande Valley Partnership

Historical Publishing Network
A division of Lammert Inc.
San Antonio, Texas

Contents

First Edition

Copyright © 2008 Historical Publishing Network and Rio Grande Valley Partnership
All rights reserved. No part of this book may be reproduced in any form or by any means, electronic or mechanical, including photocopying, without permission in writing from the publisher. All inquiries should be addressed to Historical Publishing Network, 11555 Galm Road, Suite 100, San Antonio, Texas, 78254. Phone (800) 749-9790.

ISBN: 9781893619814
Library of Congress Card Catalog Number: 2008922075

Valley Places, Valley Faces
photography by: Rebecca Rivera
text by: Eileen Mattei
profile text by: Marjorie Johnson, Eileen Mattei
design by: Vanessa Lively

Historical Publishing Network
president: Ron Lammert

project manager: Sydney McNew

administration: Donna M. Mata, Evelyn Hart, Melissa Quinn

book sales: Dee Steidle

production: Colin Hart,
Charles A. Newton III, Craig Mitchell

In the Rio Grande Valley, two cultures and two languages meet and remain linked by a shared history and a fierce attachment to their Valley home. From the tropical paradise found on the white sands of South Padre Island and Boca Chica Beach, past mesquite, live oak, citrus and palm trees, past fertile farmland and dynamic, distinctive communities to the arid brushland of western ranches, the Valley is indeed a special place. Characterized by warm weather and warm relationships, beautiful scenery enhanced by beautiful faces and the sounds of laughter, a laid-back lifestyle amid a booming economy, the Rio Grande Valley is the chosen home of nearly one million persons.

On every list of the fastest growing regions in the nation, the Valley benefits from hard-working entrepreneurs, close ties and easy access to Mexico trade, and a quality of life second to none. Driving the area's energetic evolution is the potential of the Valley's relatively young population who are being educated at two campuses of the University of Texas, numerous technical and community colleges, and by 38 school districts.

McAllen's skyline reveals how the combination of international trade, ecotourism, retail and agriculture has won the Valley's second-largest city a top spot on lists of the fastest-growing areas in the nation.

The Shary Shiver Estate recalls the citrus boom that help fuel the Valley's growth in the early 1900s.

OPPOSITE: Mercedes's reputation as the best place to go for custom-made boots is being sustained by Camargo's Western Boots which offers distinctive styles, stitching and leathers.

Many come to the Valley and stay because it is a good place to raise a family. On the other hand, the Valley is home to thousands of active retirees, both home-grown and Winter Texans. For centuries, people of all ages, ethnicities, and walks of life have been drawn to what the Valley offers.

Before the first settlers began moving north of the Rio Grande in the late 1700s to Spanish land grants named Espiritù Santo, Llano Grande, La Feria, and Concepción de Carricitios, nomadic peoples roamed the river's flood plain. At Edinburg's Museum of South Texas History, vivid, world-class exhibits bring to life the Valley's first inhabitants: the Coahuiltecans and Karankawas, Spanish explorers and pioneers, followed in time by Mexican and American ranchers and farmers.

Soon after the railroads reached the Valley 100 years ago, the Valley's population exploded as the region's natural resources were harnessed. Millions of gallons of Rio Grande water were pumped to irrigate the delta's farmland, creating a lush garden of vegetables, citrus, grains and cotton. From the north and south, people migrated to claim land and pursue their destinies. Families established home places and nourished towns, churches and civic organizations.

Today, more than ever, the Valley's physical and personal landscape is being shaped by its inhabitants as they pursue careers in medicine and manufacturing, tourism and retail, advertising and agriculture, and much more. Yet the Valley's natural resources of the Rio Grande Valley are also aiding the region's awakening. Ecotourists have discovered the Valley's unequaled bird life: red-crowned parrots, chachalacas, and buff-bellied hummingbirds, more than 512 species.

Cameron, Hidalgo, Starr, and Willacy counties stretch across 4,244 square miles of the Rio Grande Valley. Within those boundaries is a wealth of memories of yesterday and visions of tomorrow linked by the hopes and hearts of people of the Rio Grande Valley, proud to live deep in the heart of Texas.

South Padre Island's
sand, sun, and surf
make the barrier
island an irresistible
destination.

Chapter One

Living Legacy

ABOVE: Harlingen's Rialto theater celebrates The Golden Age of Hollywood & Mexican Cinema, one of the city's many murals.
BELOW: The Los Ebanos Ferry connects Mexico to Texas, three cars at a time, at the last American hand-pulled international crossing.

One of Brownsville's oldest buildings, once a mercantile establishment, the Webb-Miller house has been transformed into a contemporary art gallery.

Valley pioneers, those early ranchers and soldiers, storekeepers and settlers, established a foothold along the Rio Grande, which linked the towns of Brownsville, Roma, Hidalgo, and Rio Grande City. Relics of the 1800s have endured to become integral parts of the 21st century. In Brownsville, the gracefully-arched, weathered brick buildings of Fort Brown have been transformed into administrative offices of the University of Texas at Brownsville/Texas Southmost College. The campus's newest buildings echo the frontier architecture. A stone's throw from the Rio Grande on 13th Street, Brownsville's two oldest buildings have been lovingly restored: the 1848 Gem houses a customs broker while Galeria 409's exhibitions of contemporary border artists complement the balconied 1852 Miller-Webb building. In Edinburg, McAllen, and Brownsville, the once central railroad depots have found new lives as city and legal offices and museums. In Hidalgo, the 1910 irrigation pumphouse which sent millions of gallons of water to newly cleared brushland is again filled with the sounds of massive pumps as visitors tour the Hidalgo Pumphouse Heritage and Discovery Park. In Rio Grande City, the Laborde family's 1899 home endures as a popular inn, LaBorde House, surrounded by buildings dating from the river boat heyday. The cherished Los Ebanos ferry, the last hand-pulled ferry on a U.S. border, endures today, still moving three vehicles at a time between nations and neighborhoods. In Port Isabel, the only Texas lighthouse open to the public screens movies on its exterior for the entertainment of residents and visitors. Roma's National Historic Landmark District shelters 35 buildings more than 100 years old encircling a Hispanic-style plaza. The work of architect priest-on-horseback Pierre Keralum survives in Brownsville's Immaculate Conception Cathedral and La Lomita Mission, which gave the city of Mission its name. Harlingen Arts & Heritage Museum displays the Paso Real Stagecoach Inn, which once served the ford of the Arroyo Colorado near present day Rio Hondo. With these reminders of stone, wood, and brick, the storied past is with us.

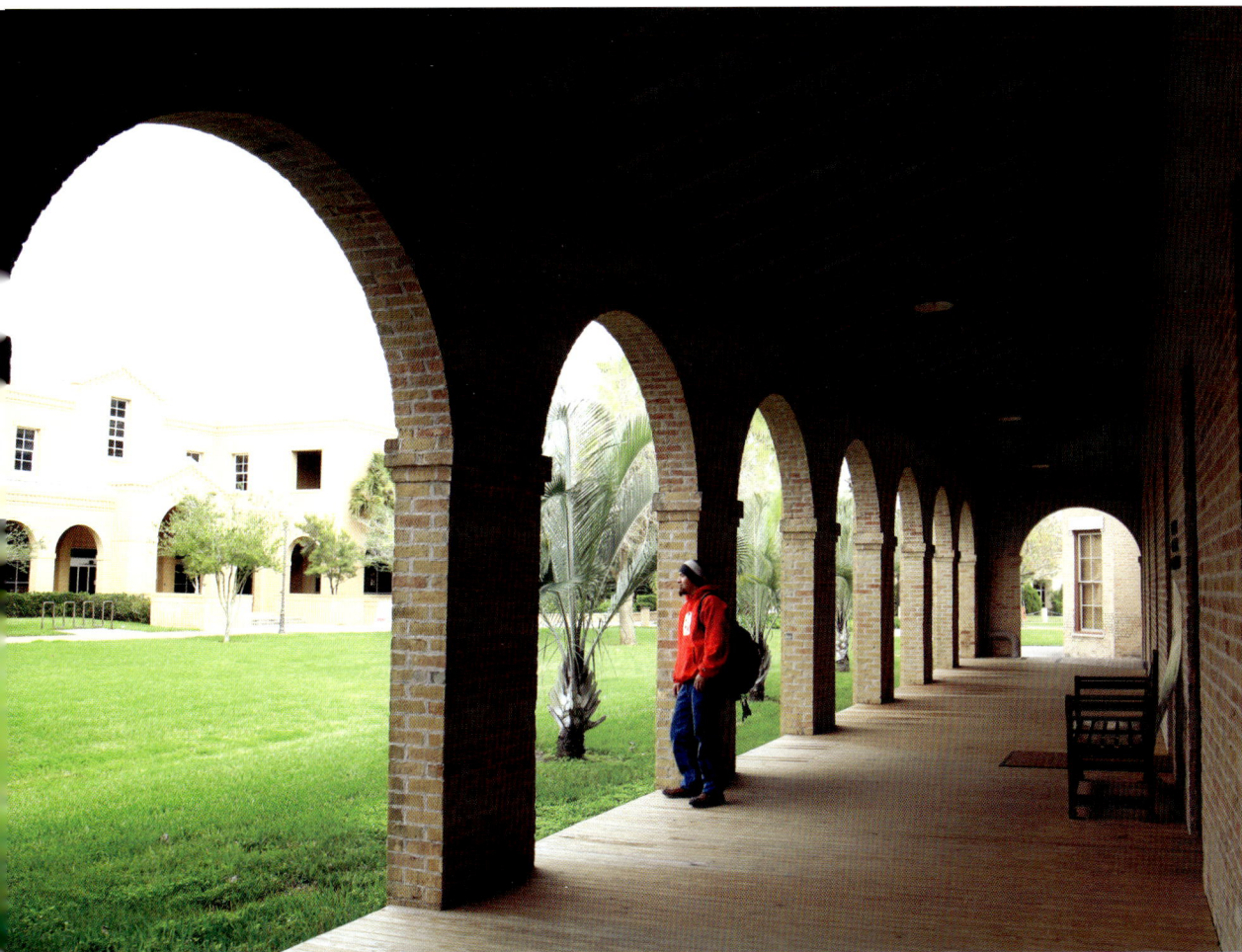

*T*he graceful arches of what was once Fort Brown's hospital now enhance the President's office at the University of Texas-Brownsville/ Texas Southmost College.

*B*rownsville's Cemetery honors early pioneers who died of cholera, yellow fever and gunshot wounds.

*T*he ruins of a Roma saloon.

*S*till in use, this Roma Bluffs building is now the office of the area's state representative.

Across the Valley, train depots have been restored to life as offices and museums.

The vaquero tradition of pan de campo lives on at Linn's Pan de Campo Festival.

Artist Mark Clark draws on Brownsville's past.

"Rock around the Clock," the signature tune of Bill Haley and the Comets, was the first rock 'n' roll record to reach Number 1. Haley, who spent his later life in Harlingen, is immortalized in a vibrant mural on Harlingen's Mural Trail which boasts over 30 historical and cultural paintings and mosaics.

*S*pines of the prickly pear may protect the cactus from animals, but humans have learned to handle the pads carefully to prepare a favorite border dish known as nopales.

*A*fter the Army closed Fort Ringgold, the barracks became classrooms for Rio Grande City's junior high school students.

Housed in a former mortuary, this art studio's doors open and close mysteriously.

Two Jima Memorial at the Marine Military Academy, Harlingen.

Built in 1865 as a way station for Oblate missionaries who visited the frontier's far-flung ranching communities, tiny La Lomita Chapel today is a cherished location for weddings.

Mothers and daughters dress up to ride on parade floats.

Chapter Two
Community

*A*BOVE: For a front row parade seat, bring your own chair.
BELOW: During Brownsville's Charro Day, youngsters celebrate Mexican traditions as their parents and grandparents did in their youth: participating in mariachi and folkloric dances.

Folkloric dancers at the University of Texas Pan American.

Each city in the Valley is composed of multiple communities representing religious, civic, recreational, educational, familial and professional interests. Yet the Rio Grande Valley itself is one big community, a state of mind and perspective. The common threads of the Valley community are revealed in festivals and family parties, school marching bands and soccer teams, and weddings and funerals too. While eating and working and playing together, people of the Valley form enduring relationships that are the basis for a community's strength and continuity. You witness community spirit in enthusiastic support of athletic and scholastic teams and in projects like cemetery cleanups and BBQs for families in need. The community's heart marches in Fourth of July parades down main street and sets neighborhoods twinkling with Christmas lights. The community celebrates with quinceaneras and with pinatas at birthdays parties on the patio. Festivals reflect a city's distinct personality and sense of fun. Where else but Weslaco for the Onion Festival, where the 1015 onion was developed? Abundant sand and sunshine energize South Padre's Sandcastle Days. Just add cowboys and horses to Los Fresnos arena to conjure up the annual PCRA Rodeo. San Benito's Narciso Martinez Conjunto Festival tempts elderly couples and young ones to the dance floor. In Hidalgo, BorderFest recognizes the many different cultures that have influenced the Valley. Brownsville has celebrated Charro Days for 70 years, renewing its relationship with its sister city Matamoros, and launched the Latin Jazz Festival for more dancing in the streets. Everywhere towns put their best foot forward for fiesta time: Mission's Citrus Festival, McAllen's Texas Tropics Nature Festival, Harlingen's Jackson Street Jubilee, Mercedes' Rio Grande Valley Livestock Show and Rodeo. Communities host softball tournaments, bicycle rides and motorcycle rallies while organizations arrange parades, carnivals and charity walkathons. Museums like International Museum of Art & Science, Costumes of the Americas, the Iwo Jima Memorial, and the Brownsville Heritage Complex open vistas on art, science, history and cultures. Community and touring theater, mariachi bands, blues and country singers, orchestras and chorales, all open the eyes and ears of audiences to the world beyond the Valley.

Our Lady of Lourdes Grotto in Rio Grande City.

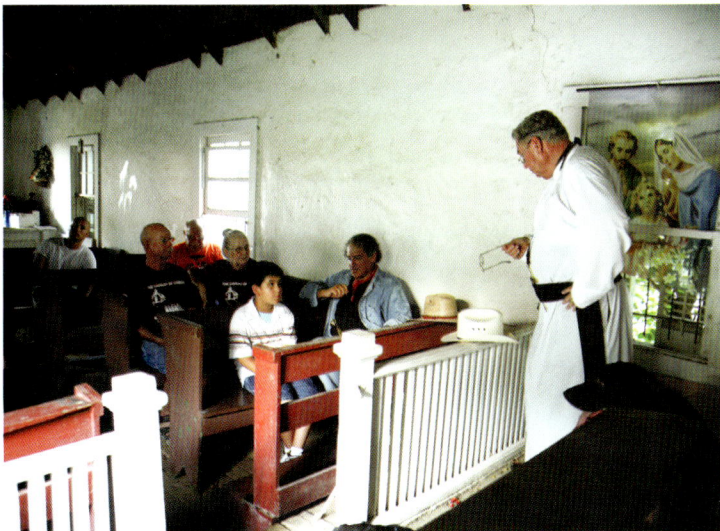

Father Roy Snipes brings a message of Christian brotherhood.

Delicious, hot off the spit into a tortilla: that's a real Valley taco!

Fun + Foods = Festivals.

Proud to serve their country, many young Valley men and women join the military.

ABOVE: Hidalgo turned the notoriety of having the nation's first killer bees into an asset. **O**PPOSITE: The Killer Bees introduced ice hockey to the Valley and now draw big crowds to Dodge Arena.

ishing the jetties at Isla Blanca.

Children consider face painting a must-do at Valley festivals. Mission's Butterfly Festival invites youngsters to be part of the celebration of natural wonders.

Weslaco-birthplace of the 1015 onion and the Onion Festival.

THE UNIVERSITY OF TEXAS - PAN AMERICAN

The University of Texas Pan American, which grew from Edinburg College founded in 1927, today is the tenth largest university in Texas with over 17,000 students. It educates more Mexican-Americans than any other university in the nation.

The Rio Grande Valley Dorados bring action-packed Arena Football to Hidalgo's Dodge Arena April through August.

*T*he Valley's diverse cultures encompass the world's religions. Traditions run deep as grandfathers flank a young man at his Bar Mitzvah at Beth Israel Temple in Harlingen.

The Rio Grande Valley's rich natural assets of butterflies, birds and native plants add to the region's beauty, while attracting ecotourists to observe flora and fauna found nowhere else in the country.

Chapter Three

Treasures &
Pleasures

ABOVE: The region's largest
public art collection fills
Harlingen's library and
library courtyard.
BELOW: Music...
movement...dance.

𝟽 he Harlingen Arts &
Heritage museum
intersperses exhibits
of contemporary
artists with cultural
displays such as Day
of the Dead and
historical landmarks
like the Paso Real
Stagecoach Inn.

𝖮 PPOSITE: Golfing
year-round on
numerous courses is
one of the benefits
of life in the Rio
Grande Valley.

The Rio Grande Valley offers exceptional pleasures – sensual experiences – made possible by its distinctive natural resources. Fishing on the placid Laguna Madre, the Mother Bay. Listening to red-crowned parrots squawking in a live oak tree heavy with acorns. Picking fragrant Ruby Red grapefruit. Feeling the breeze in the lacy shade of a mesquite tree. Canoeing the Rio Grande. Eating white wing doves prepared in a succulent rosemary-tomato sauce. Watching black-bellied whistling ducks line up on a suburban roof. Being dazzled by landscapes overflowing with magenta bougainvillea, lemon yellow hibiscus and tropical palms.

Plants and wildlife of the Valley frequently are described with the phrase "found nowhere else in the U.S." Increasingly, ecotourists flock to the Valley to see the birds common to our neighborhoods and fields, such as great kiskadees and green parakeets, as well as less common species like hook billed kites and pygmy owls. Ecotourism is thriving, in part, because of the concerted restoration of native habitat (once called weeds) in areas such as Harlingen's Ramsey Nature Park, a former landfill transformed by volunteers into a 40-acre birding and plant sanctuary. Edinburg Scenic Wetlands and World Birding Center, at the city reservoir, hosts spectacular butterfly gardens, while Valley Nature Center in Weslaco is a surprising jungle of native habitat in an urban setting. Laguna Atascosa and Santa Ana National Wildlife Refuges have gained renown for their diverse species: jaguarundis, ocelots, alligators, and roseate spoonbills. The much-loved Gladys Porter Zoo provides a walk on the wild side for the less adventurous.

Along the Gulf of Mexico, the sand and waves of South Padre Island that bring the excitement of body surfing and sandcastle building to some visitors offers moments of tranquility and shell seeking to others. More treasures of the Laguna Madre are revealed on dolphin watching cruises and by wading anglers. Naturally, the tropical habitat and climate invites athletes–golfers, runners, soccer players–to enjoy their sports year round. Truly the Rio Grande Valley is the definition of the great outdoors.

*F*ragrant, fresh
citrus fruit...
a privilege of
Valley life.

A Spanish caravel, like this one at the Museum of South Texas History, can still launch dreams.

$\mathcal{F}$amous for its tamales, the De Alba Bakery also makes delicious and colorful Mexican pastries known as pan dulce.

A potent Cosmopolitan symbolizes the Rio Grande Valley's increasingly urban and international outlook.

*f*abulous tiles adorn Quinta Mazatlan, a 1930's hacienda with tropical gardens that now is the centerpiece of McAllen's World Birding Center.

*G*ladys Porter Zoo.

*T*he International Museum of Art & Science introduces McAllen children to the wonders of nature, including iguanas.

*M*ission's extensive bicycle trails let a father and son escape the bustle of traffic and enjoy the outdoors together.

The Children's Museum in Brownsville entertains and educates simultaneously.

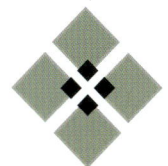

*Q*ueen Isabella Memorial Causeway gets visits from pelicans who fish the Laguna Madre.

Sea Ranch Marina on South Padre provides a berth for yachts and fishing boats as well as a departure point for tours of the bay to watch dolphins and sunsets.

The only Texas lighthouse open to the public, the Port Isabel Lighthouse State Historic Site was built in 1853. Visitors who climb the spiral staircase to the top get a view of the coastal plains and the Laguna Madre.

Butterfly watching is becoming as popular as bird watching in the Valley with ecotourists flocking to Mission's annual Butterfly Festival and the nearby North American Butterfly Association Park.

Cleaning the day's catch on a dock of the bay.

Spanish treasure ships sank off the beaches of South Padre centuries ago. Visitors today find the white sand beach is itself a stunning treasure.

*T*he woods of Quinta Mazatlan shelter beautiful semi-tropical birds like red-crowned parrots, great kiskadees, and chachalacas.

Chapter Four
Enterprise

*A*BOVE: Valley processing plants receive tons of citrus daily during the season.
BELOW: Bell's Farm to Market keeps its tomatoes healthy.
OPPOSITE: A reminder of aviation's early days greets travelers at McAllen Miller International Airport bound for international and U.S. destinations.

The logisitics industry- trucking, warehousing and distributing components and finished products to and from Mexico- is a major contributor to the region's booming economy. Dozens of international corporations such as Panasonic, Black & Decker, and Seagate Technologies operate border plants and logistics centers.

Diversification of the economy has allowed the Valley to weather bad times, bad weather and peso devaluation. Manufacturers– no longer labor intensive – prosper and expand by using high-tech equipment and highly-skilled employees. AMFELS employs more than 1,000 to fabricate and repair towering ocean going oil rigs. Both Texas' largest shrimp fleet and 1,500 acres of shrimp farms call Cameron County home. Just like 100 years ago, when the new railroad enabled farmers to ship their produce and fruit to distant markets, commerce today revolves around logistics. The economy continues to expand because of access to Mexico, newly-rebuilt highways, major airports in McAllen, Harlingen and Brownsville, ports in Brownsville, Port Isabel and Harlingen, and international bridges for commercial traffic and business and leisure travelers. Healthcare ranges from technology-based digital imaging centers and specialty hospitals to long-term care facilities and mobile screening vans. The Regional Academic Health Center, a campus of the University of Texas San Antonio Health Science Center, provides third and fourth year medical students with hands-on training in Harlingen, while a public health arm operates in Brownsville, and a medical research wing is taking on projects in Edinburg. The RAHC focuses much of its training and research on problems of the border population: diabetes, heart disease and certain infectious diseases. Farming and ranching, cotton gins and packing houses, continue to be potent forces in the Valley. While a

farm may have been in a family for generations, things are being done differently than in grandpa's time. A new end-product of cotton production is bio-fuel, a product of the innovative bio-energy plant at the Valley's cottonseed oil mill. Santa Rosa's sugar cane mill, the last in Texas, is generating almost all its electrical power from cane waste. Water-wise drip irrigation conserves the Valley's most limited resource. Mercedes' new outlet mall proved that retail is alive and well, drawing shoppers from across the region and Mexico. Around the Valley construction firms, bakeries, boutiques and hundreds of enterprises keep joining the animated business world, meeting demands, creating new demands.

A rancher checks his cattle held in a *corral de leña*.

*P*umped from the Rio Grande, irrigation water flows over flat fields of cotton, grain and vegetables to turn the Valley green.

*R*oadside farm stands and street vendors share the Valley's bounty of sweet onions, peppers, limes, and tomatoes.

McAllen Regional Hospital, the Edinburg World Birding Center and Rio Grande Premium Outlets in Mercedes represent three strong and booming sectors of the Valley's economy: healthcare, ecotourism, and retail.

*K*nown as relief in a leaf, aloe vera helps heal burns and wounds and is included in hundreds of lotions and cosmetics. The Valley is one of two places in the United States where aloe vera is grown.

Shrimp trawlers berthed at Port Isabel and the Port of Brownsville comprise the nation's largest shrimping fleet.

The new McAllen Convention Center blends Spanish and Mediterranean architecture with tropical landscaping in creating expansive meeting spaces and a multi-use park.

Chapter Five
Faces

ABOVE: Family time.
BELOW: Shriners raise money to help crippled children
OPPOSITE: Hair styles may come and go, but, friendly, hometown service has never gone out of style at Mission's oldest barbershop.

SHRINERS HOSPITALS FOR CHILDREN
1-800-237-5055

The Rio Grande Valley's history has been shaped by names still familiar: Yturria, Balli, de la Garza, McAllen, Young, Hill, Vela, Robertson, Champion, Mussina, Vale. More than just legends, those names are carried by their descendants who apply contemporary viewpoints as they in turn strive to shape the Rio Grande Valley into a better place. Beyond the famous names, so many others have contributed to making the Valley what it is today: a place of warm abrazzos and true family values, with an appreciation of the tropical climate and remarkable natural resources. Legacies for future generations are being shaped across the Rio Grande Valley. To see tomorrow's promise, look in the faces you'll find in these communities: Hidalgo, McAllen, Mission, Edinburg, Sullivan City, Los Fresnos, Brownsville, Port Isabel, Laguna Vista, Harlingen, Raymondville, La Feria, Santa Rosa, La Villa, Mercedes, Weslaco, Elsa-Edcouch, Hargill, Lasara, Alamo, San Juan, Pharr, La Joya, Rio Grande City, Roma, Raymondville, Sebastian, Lyford, Los Indios, Bluetown, Las Yescas, San Perlita, Port Mansfield, Monte Alto, Santa Maria.

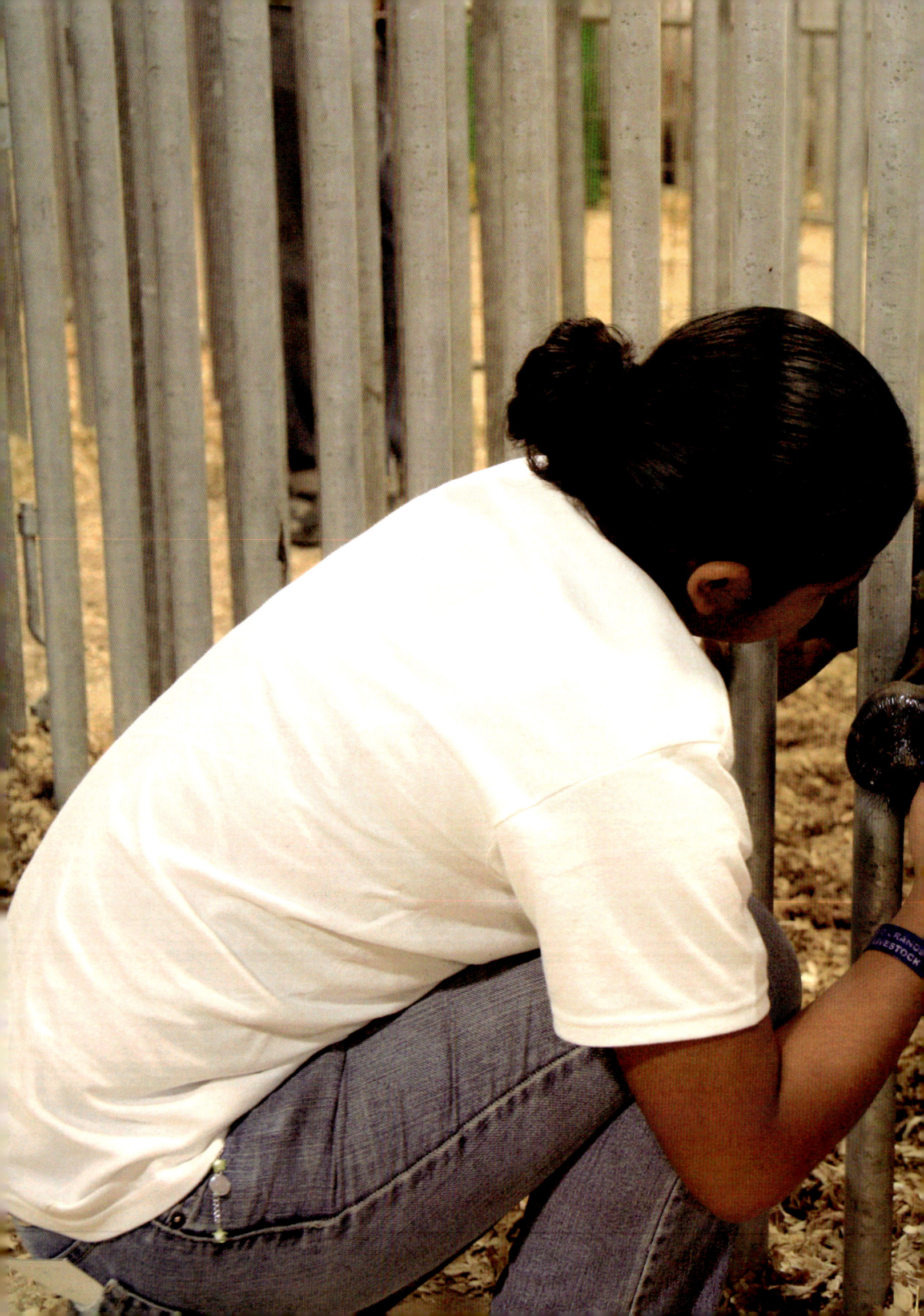

ABOVE: A Valley tradition, fragrant pan dulce includes gingerbread pigs and pastries shaped like little ears and little shells.

OPPOSITE TOP: Surfers-to-be hone their skills in the waves of South Padre Island.

OPPOSITE BOTTOM: Colorful fruit flavors top the shaved ice treats known as raspas.

More and more Valley high school graduates are heading to colleges and universities to pursue their career dreams.

*S*haring an abrazzo.

*F*ood tempts Winter Texans and residents alike.

Pre-k kids learn about lobsters at H-E-B grocery store.

Not home cooking.

*S*alsa, Two-step, rock n roll: the Valley loves to dance the night away.

*A*n evening out with friends.

*A*BOVE: Friday night in Sharyland
OPPOSITE: Corn on the cob - or elotes: a sweet but messy treat at Valley festivals.

*V*alley high school bands strut their stuff and their songs at the Pigskin Jubilee.

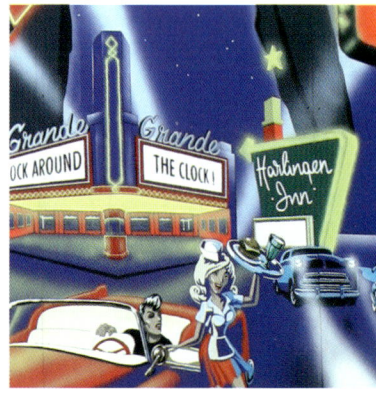

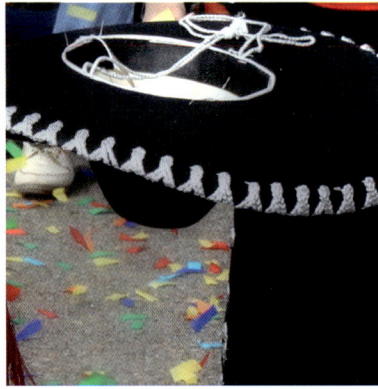

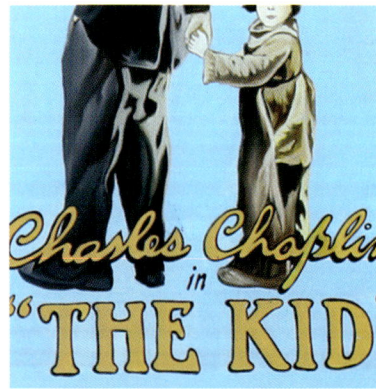

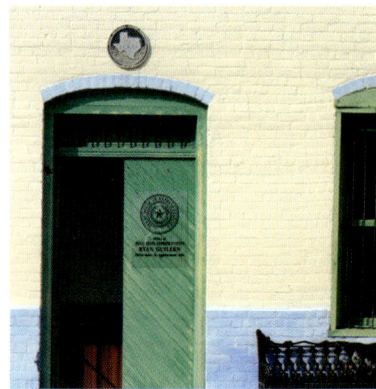

Valley Partners

historic profiles of businesses, organizations, and families that have contributed to the development and economic base of the Rio Grande Valley

Special Thanks to:

Driscoll Children's Hospital

Valley Grande Institute for Academic Studies

South Padre Island Convention & Visitors Bureau

CATHOLIC DIOCESE OF BROWNSVILLE

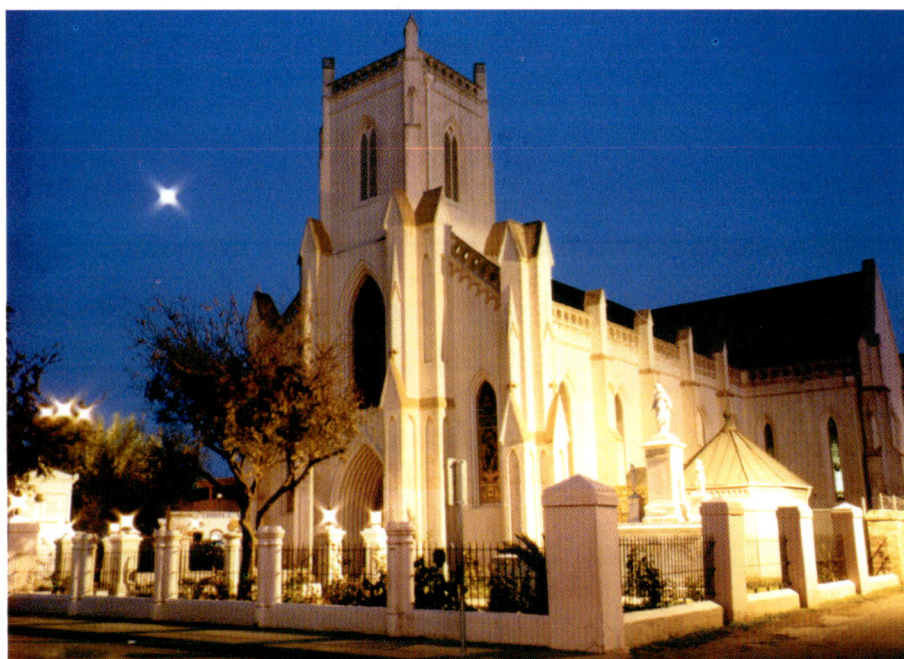

Above: La Lomita Chapel in Mission.

Below: Immaculate Conception Cathedral in Brownsville.

Before the Rio Grande River served as a border between two countries, the Catholic faith became an integral part of the life and history of the Rio Grande Valley. Originally it was under the ecclesiastical jurisdiction of the bishop of Guadalajara and later that of the bishop of Linares. During this time, the Franciscan Friars were among the first responsible for the evangelization of the residents of the area and the pastoral care of the Catholic community.

After Texas joined the Union in 1845 the Diocese of Galveston was founded in 1847 to oversee the immense territory covering the entire State of Texas. With 20,000 Catholics in the area, the responsibility to serve them was taken on by Jean Marie Odin, C.M., the Bishop of Galveston, and about nine priests.

On September 18, 1874, Pope Pius IX established the Vicariate Apostolic of Brownsville, with the Immaculate Conception Church chosen as Cathedral. This new ecclesiastical area had its own bishop, who was called a Vicar Apostolic. The Vicariate, essentially a missionary territory, encompassed what are now the Diocese of Brownsville, the Diocese of Corpus Christi, and the Diocese of Laredo. This area included by far the largest population adhering to the Roman Catholic Faith, but was small in resources when compared to Galveston and San Antonio.

By the third quarter of the nineteenth century Roman Catholics in the Vicariate of Brownsville numbered about 42,000, many of whom lived in the counties of Cameron, Willacy, Hidalgo and Starr, which today constitute the Diocese of Brownsville.

Raising livestock was the major industry, and isolated settlements of ranchers and their families, friends and servants were served by the Oblates of Mary Immaculate who arrived in December 1849 at the invitation of the Bishop of Galveston. They were temporarily withdrawn in 1851, but returned in 1852. One of the first Oblates who arrived in the Valley, Father Alexander Sourlerin, spearheaded the "pony" ranch ministry. Each week he faithfully mounted his pony and set out to remote ranches with his Mass kit daring the dangers and privations of a 3,600 square mile frontier territory. The Oblates' traveling by horseback earned them the name of the "Cavalry of Christ."

Father Dominic Manucy, a priest from the Diocese of Mobile, was the first bishop selected to serve the Brownsville Vicariate. Installed in the Immaculate Conception Cathedral in Brownsville on February 14, 1874, he labored tirelessly over the next nine years, until his transfer to the Diocese of Mobile in 1884. He later asked to be allowed to return to the Brownsville Vicariate; however, he died before he was able to return.

Father Claude C. Jaillet, Vicar General of the Vicariate, served as administrator, until Father Pedro Verdaguer was appointed in 1890 as Bishop of the Vicariate Apostolic of Brownsville.

From ox carts and burro trains, transportation advanced around the middle of the nineteenth century to steamboats plying the Rio Grande and overland freight transport via mule-drawn wagons. The real advance came a bit later, however, with

Priests of the Diocese of Brownsville at the Chrism Mass.

completion of a rail line linking the Lower Rio Grande Valley to the rest of North America. By the 1920s almost every major community in the present Diocese of Brownsville had a railroad station. A combination of the improved transportation situation and development of irrigation that fostered agricultural development along the Valley brought an influx of settlers to the area.

Many improvements were made in the Vicariate during this period, including the construction of St. Peter's Church in Laredo in 1896, to serve English-speaking Catholics of that area, and construction of Our Lady of Guadalupe Church in 1899 in Mission, to meet the needs of the growing Mexican-American population. Between 1908 and 1910 Catholic churches were built in Harlingen and Raymondville, and as new towns were established, additional mission centers and chapels were added.

Early efforts to enlist women's religious communities in France to work in the area were unsuccessful until four sisters of the Incarnate Word and Blessed Sacrament agreed to come to Texas in 1852. Remaining in Galveston for several months to learn English and Spanish, they then sailed to Brownsville, where they lived in a small, one-story warehouse until a new convent and boarding school for girls was constructed. Named the Incarnate Word Academy, it was to become the oldest school for girls in Texas. The sisters faced a succession of crises ranging from epidemics, tropical storms and Civil War clashes to the death of one sister in an Indian attack. Through it all, they not only persevered but actually extended their service throughout the Dioceses of Galveston and San Antonio. In 1900, they opened a school which operated for more than twenty years in Rio Grande City.

Other women's religious communities, including the Order of the Sisters of Mercy, the Sisters of the Sacred Heart of Jesus, the Sisters of the Holy Ghost and Mary Immaculate, the Sisters of Divine Providence, the Sisters of St. Joseph, the Sisters of St. Joseph of Bourg, and the Sisters of St. Joseph of Carondolet, also have long histories of service to people in the Lower Rio Grande Valley. They have operated Catholic schools and taught in several public schools over a long period, as well as teaching

Above: Basilica of Our Lady of San Juan del Valle-National Shrine.

Below: The Oblates of Mary Immaculate were one of the first religious orders to serve the people of the Rio Grande Valley. They first arrived in 1849 and traveled by horseback to celebrate Mass at the remote ranches.

catechism. A number of other orders have also served in Confraternity of Christian Doctrine programs and the home visiting apostolate in the present Diocese of Brownsville.

By 1911 the Brownsville Vicariate had 16 diocesan, 16 religious order priests, 15 churches with resident pastors, and 60 chapels and mission centers attended by the overworked missionaries. The following year it was converted into the Diocese of Corpus Christi, with St. Patrick's Church in Corpus Christi to be the Bishop's Cathedral. This diocese had a population of 158,000, among them were 83,000 Catholics. Catholic organizations, retreats, missions and devotions were established, and in his first Confirmation tour, the Bishop confirmed almost 1,000 people in Brownsville and over 500 more in San Benito. Emphasis on education led to the opening of quality parochial schools in Harlingen, Mercedes, San Benito, and elsewhere, as well as the establishment of a number of additional churches. By 1919 the Catholic Church's presence in the Diocese had grown to 46 priests, 31 churches with resident priests and 83 missions and chapels. These served 99,580 Catholics.

With an influx of Catholic immigrants of widely varied heritage—German, Polish, Irish, and Mexican—parishes, church improvements and schools were added during the next four decades. On July 10, 1965, Pope Paul VI established the Diocese of Brownsville, with Bishop Adolph Marx installed on September 2, 1965, at the Cathedral of Brownsville. This 4,226-square-mile area contained 40 parishes, 46 missions and 22 stations, served by 14 diocesan priests and 67 Religious Order priests. Bishop Marx died not long after his installation; he was succeeded by Bishop Humberto S. Medeiros.

During the turbulent sixties, a period of unrest throughout the country, the Brownsville Diocese faced hard issues, including violence between farm workers and farm owners in Starr County. Bishop Medeiros, who was later named Archbishop of Boston, offered his services as mediator in the dispute, and urged his own parishioners and the bishops of northern areas to provide for both the secular and religious needs of the migrant workers.

Bishop John J. Fitzpatrick, a native of Canada, was appointed the third Bishop of Brownsville on April 27, 1971. He served the Diocese for twenty years until his retirement on November 30, 1991.

During his tenure, Bishop Fitzpatrick upheld the dignity and rights of the poor and oppressed, whether they were farm workers, migrant laborers, Central American refugees or farmers caught in financial difficulties. Because of the unbelievably lopsided ratio of parishioners per priest he promoted the lay ministry programs. He also purchased and maintained a public broadcasting station in the Valley for the service of the community.

Upon Bishop Fitzpatrick's retirement, Bishop Enrique San Pedro, S.J., was installed as the fourth bishop of Brownsville. He placed the need to improve the quality of education as his first priority in the Diocese. Sadly his time was cut short with his unexpected death on July 17, 1994.

Continued growth of the Lower Rio Grande Valley during the last half of the twentieth century and into the twenty-first century along with the increased number of Catholics in the Brownsville Diocese, has encouraged cooperative efforts and the use of modern technology in handling diocesan business matters to allow priests to concentrate their efforts on the most important of their duties to the faithful. The increasing burden of work on the religious community has also resulted in increased reliance on the laity in promoting works of the church, as well as an intensive program promoting vocations to the priesthood. All of these measures are designed to serve the Diocese's more than 850,000 Catholics; these growing numbers have led to the establishment of seven new parishes. Six of these were established under the leadership of Bishop Raymundo J. Peña, who was installed on August 6, 1995 as the fifth bishop of Brownsville.

The deeply religious nature of Catholics in the Brownsville Diocese is expressed in many ways, including the Shrine of Our Lady of San Juan del Valle. This shrine now delivers its message of faith to more than 80,000 Catholics each month. Originally a small wooden chapel in San Juan, the site drew so many pilgrims that a shrine was built and officially dedicated in 1954. The new church was destroyed in a fire on October 23, 1970 when a pilot crashed into the structure. A beautiful new shrine was dedicated in 1980. Pope John Paul II designated the Shrine as a minor basilica in 1999.

Under Bishop Peña's leadership, the First Diocesan Synod was convoked on June 10, 2000, and celebrated to identify the pastoral priorities, initiatives and strategies that would promote and sustain the mission of the Church in the Rio Grande Valley.

Responding to the Synod's call, the diocese has opened a junior college level seminary, an Institute for the formation of lay ministers, a permanent deacon formation program, a medical clinic to serve the poor, a tuition-free middle school for gifted students of low-income households, an

office for immigration and refugee services and a Chapel of Adoration of the Blessed Sacrament, with the adjoining monastery of Poor Clare Nuns.

Also the rigorous promotion of vocations has resulted in an increase in the number of seminarians, and new priests have been ordained each year in the Diocese. Since 1996, Bishop Peña has ordained twenty-five new priests. With a continued focus on vocations, the Diocese and the Pontifical College Josephinum from Columbus, Ohio, entered into a collaborative effort in 2001 to open the Saint Joseph and Saint Peter Seminary. The junior college seminary in La Lomita south of Mission is located on the grounds of St. Peter's Novitiate, the former novitiate of the Oblates of Mary Immaculate.

As Bishop Peña wrote in his pastoral letter following the first Diocesan Synod, "Our particular church is coming of age. We are gradually transforming our mission diocese into a missionary diocese. As we reflect on the humble, yet vibrant, beginnings of the Church in the Rio Grande Valley, we look to a future full of hope."

Above: Bishop Raymundo J. Peña meets with Pope Benedict XVI during a pilgrimage to the Vatican.

Below: Four men are ordained to the priesthood during a Mass at the Basilica of Our Lady of San Juan del Valle-National Shrine.

HIDALGO INDEPENDENT SCHOOL DISTRICT

Below: The current Hidalgo ISD Central Office and Annex Buildings are the oldest school houses in Hidalgo County. The structure below was built in the 1890s and once housed students from elementary on to high school.

PHOTOGRAPH BY ARIANNA VAZQUEZ.

The history of the Hidalgo Independent School District can be traced to the mid 1800s, shortly after Texas joined the Union. During that time, the community of Hidalgo established education as a priority. It is believed its citizens established the first school in 1852.

Not long afterwards, the first permanent schoolhouse was built. This "two-room schoolhouse" is still in use today and is the oldest standing educational facility in Hidalgo County. The outlying communities of Junco, Capote and Granjeno, also established schools during that time, operating together as one common school district under the direction of the county. A two-story school building added in the 1890s eventually housed about ten classrooms from elementary to high school. This historical building serves as the district's central office and Board of Trustees meeting room today.

It was not until 1925, that the state legislature designated these local schools as the Hidalgo Independent School District, encompassing thirty-six square miles running parallel to the Rio Grande River.

The district's present day boundaries include the original town site of Hidalgo, most of Granjeno, portions of McAllen, Pharr, and extended rural areas. Most students in the district live in Hidalgo or Hidalgo Park (a sector of the Las Milpas area in south Pharr).

A few students come from Granjeno or other rural neighborhoods and farms.

Hidalgo ISD grew slowly from 1925 to 1975. The population was relatively stable and consisted of families engaged in agriculture and to a lesser extent, commerce. After decades of proudly celebrating high school graduations, Hidalgo ISD found it increasingly difficult to bear the expense of operating a high school with the small number of students available. In the 1950s the district made arrangements to transport high school students to McAllen ISD for their studies. Meanwhile, continued growth resulted in the construction of a new campus for elementary and junior high students. This

building, opened in 1960, houses Hidalgo Elementary today.

In the 1970s, responding to climbing enrollment, the Board of Trustees decided that Hidalgo could once again afford to operate its own high school. In 1976, Hidalgo High School opened its doors, serving grades seven to twelve. In 1978, Hidalgo ISD celebrated graduation ceremonies for the first time in more than two decades.

Hidalgo ISD continued to grow throughout the 1980s, adding a separate junior high campus (Ida Diaz Junior High), and a second elementary school (J.C. Kelly Elementary) to accommodate the growth in the Las Milpas area.

The year 1991 marked the beginning of two decades of facility expansion and enhancement. During this time, the community voted overwhelmingly in favor of six bond elections, authorizing a total of more than $50 million in facility improvements.

Several new wings have been added to the high school, including modern science and computer labs, fine arts classrooms, a spacious band hall, and a large gymnasium. New wings have been added to the junior high campus, including science labs, a new band hall, a new cafeteria, and a new library. A new library and

several new wings were added to J.C. Kelly Elementary. The district also added its third elementary, Dr. Alejo Salinas, Jr. Elementary, which opened its doors in the fall of 1999. A fourth new elementary, Hidalgo Park opened in 2004. A new Hidalgo Elementary facility will open its doors in 2007, replacing a campus that is almost fifty years old.

As a result of this aggressive construction schedule, the district alleviated overcrowding

Since the 1960s, and every decade in between, Hidalgo ISD has undergone some sort of expansion to meet the demands of growth within the school district. Hidalgo ISD currently has close to 3,500 students in its four elementary campuses, a junior high, an alternative campus and a high school.

PHOTOGRAPHS BY ARIANNA VAZQUEZ.

and the use of old portable buildings at the campuses. Today every classroom and educational facility in the district is new (less than ten years old) or recently remodeled. Improvements have been made in support areas as well. The district constructed new buildings for the maintenance and transportation departments, and a new central kitchen. The current decade has seen the student population continue to increase at a slow, but steady pace. In 2002-03, student membership surpassed 3,000 for the first time ever, and by 2007 was approaching 3,500. The emphasis on facilities enhancement has continued.

Although the student growth and facilities improvements at Hidalgo ISD have been phenomenal in recent years, it is academics that have made the district shine.

Hidalgo ISD has established a reputation for excellence and represents one of the best educational systems in the State of Texas. In 2001 the district became one of the few to have achieved the coveted Exemplary designation on the state's rigorous accountability system. Even rarer was the fact that all campuses also achieved this level. Up to the year 2006, Hidalgo ISD has been an either Recognized or Exemplary school district for nine consecutive years and is working to continue to make history, as the district enters a second decade of continuous academic excellence.

Currently designated a Recognized district, Hidalgo ISD boasts student performance equal to or above state and regional averages at all grade levels. Hidalgo ISD has also excelled in the realm of extracurricular activities, winning two state marching band championships, numerous district and playoff crowns in athletics and various literary competitions. In all arenas, Hidalgo ISD is recognized for excellence.

In 2005, Hidalgo ISD was a finalist for the H-E-B Excellence in Education Award, designating it one of the five best school districts in Texas. That same year, Hidalgo High School was named one of the best high schools in Texas by the Texas Educational Excellence Project for quality and equity in educating all

students. The high school became nationally recognized that year, as well. At the elementary level, J.C. Kelly Elementary was honored with the TEBC/JFTK Honor roll for sustained whole-school academic excellence in Texas.

Challenging the assumption that minority students living in an environment of poverty cannot excel, Hidalgo ISD has caught the attention of many educators and experts at the state and national levels. In the spring of 2005, Hidalgo ISD and the University of Texas System received two grants totaling $1.2 million from the Bill and Melinda Gates Foundation to transform Hidalgo High School into an Early College High School over a five-year time frame. The goal is to have all students "college ready" and enrolled in college during their junior and senior years in high school. The senior class of 2010 will be the first class to graduate from the Hidalgo Early College High School.

Hidalgo ISD receives visits from school districts, universities, and researchers from all over the country. The district has been featured by major news media at the state level and in several national publications as well. Hidalgo ISD's secret to success is simple, but rare. Hidalgo ISD boasts outstanding, dedicated teachers and staff working in a supportive, politically stable community, led by a visionary, committed Board of Trustees. Students are eager and talented and parental support is exceptional. All of these ingredients are combined through a Total Team Effort to create an Exemplary Educational System: One Student at a Time, following a No Excuses: philosophy.

In 2006, Hidalgo ISD received the H-E-B Excellence in Education Award, recognized as the best school district in Texas, and received a cash prize of $100,000. In that same year, Hidalgo High School was named one of the three best performing high schools in Texas based on a national study done by Just for the Kids and sponsored by the National Center for Education Accountability (NCEA). Another study by Standard & Poor's rated Hidalgo High School one of the best in the nation. Hidalgo ISD also received unique recognition from Teach the Children, a national nonprofit organization, during their Twenty-third Annual Teach the Children Telethon KRGV-TV Channel

5, for the school district's work in motivating and teaching disadvantaged students.

The Hidalgo ISD Board of Trustees was named as a Texas Association of School Administrators (TASA) State Honor Board in 2006. The Superintendent of Schools, Dr. Daniel P. King, was named the Texas Association of School Boards (TASB) Superintendent of the Year.

It has truly been an upward journey that will only get better. The rich history of Hidalgo ISD continues to be written by its students, faculty and staff every day. As a result of their hard work and dedication, Hidalgo ISD is the Treasure on the Border.

Hidalgo ISD continues to exceed expectations because of its number one philosophy of always placing students first regardless of their background. In Hidalgo ISD, all students have the ability and opportunity to succeed.

PHOTOGRAPH BY ARIANNA VAZQUEZ.

VALLEY BAPTIST HEALTH SYSTEM

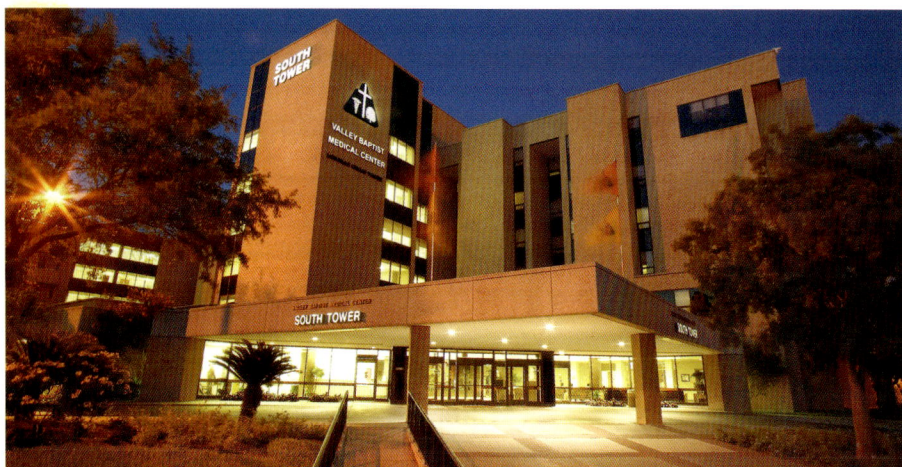

Above: Dr. Rick Bassett has pioneered the development of new joint replacement prostheses at Valley Baptist Medical Center.

Below: Valley Baptist Medical Center-Harlingen has been serving the Valley with quality, compassionate care since 1925.

Much more than two outstanding hospitals, Valley Baptist Health System offers comprehensive healthcare service to the communities it serves. A regional healthcare leader dedicated to health and wellness for people at all stages of life, Valley Baptist has earned a stellar reputation for patient care, community service, corporate citizenship, commitment to quality, and excellence in operations. By reaching out to the community with free health screenings and health information, a locally-owned health plan, home health and hospice services, advanced diagnostics and imaging facilities, and with ambulatory surgical centers, a skilled nursing facility, and more, Valley Baptist has become a Regional Integrated Delivery System and the largest health system in Cameron County.

Anchoring the health system are its two first-class, acute care inpatient facilities: Valley Baptist Medical Center-Harlingen and Valley Baptist Medical Center-Brownsville. Both hospitals trace their roots back to dedicated doctors, visionary citizens, and Christian organizations. In Harlingen, Valley Baptist Medical Center-Harlingen traces its roots to the thirty-six-bed Valley Baptist Hospital, opened on "F" Street in 1925 by the Lower Rio Grande Valley Baptist Association. In 1956 the hospital opened its present location to become the heart of a medical district encircled by physician offices and outpatient services including Treasure Hills Imaging Center, Advanced Medical Supply, and Golden Palms Retirement and Health Center.

In Brownsville, Divine Providence Hospital managed by the Sisters of Mercy opened in

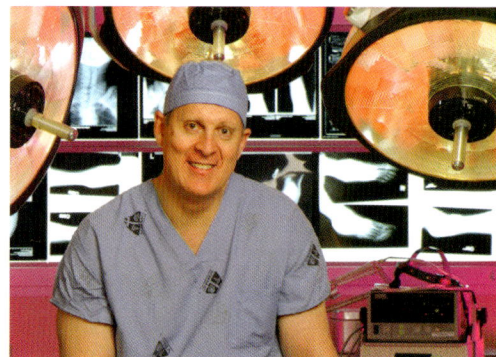

1917, leading to Mercy Hospital in 1923. The hospital was renamed Brownsville Medical Center in 1974 and joined the Valley Baptist family in 2004 as Valley Baptist Medical Center-Brownsville.

For years, Valley Baptist has led the way in responsive, modern medical care. The Rio Grande Valley's first open heart surgery and cardiac catheterization procedures were performed at Valley Baptist Medical Center-Harlingen, which also welcomed the region's first Joint Replacement Center, the first dedicated Children's Center, and South Texas' first Level III Trauma Center. VBMC-Brownsville, which is also a Level III Trauma Center, has an accredited diabetes education center, along with its sister hospital. With all-digital imaging at VBMC-Brownsville, VBMC-Harlingen and the Treasure Hills Imaging Center, the results of diagnostic imaging tests are accessible to physicians almost instantaneously, enabling patient treatments to begin sooner.

The region's only locally owned and operated health plan, Valley Baptist Health Plans has received a ninety-five percent member satisfaction rating, as well as an award for its comprehensive diabetes management measures. (The satisfaction rating is based on surveys of health plan members by Valley Baptist Health Plans.) With a network of over 575 physicians and eight hospitals, Valley Baptist Health Plans offers a health insurance menu designed to meet every need of large and small employers, individuals and Medicare/Medicaid beneficiaries. Until recently, most people in the Valley had little choice but to enroll in an out-of-state national insurance plan. Now, through Valley Baptist Health Plans, Valley residents can select a locally owned and

operated health plan—one that understands who they are and where they live.

Valley Baptist Health Plans offers three Valley Advantage plans designed for Medicare patients. And Valley Baptist Health Plans offers Valley Advantage Select, a plan solely for individuals who are Medicare and Medicaid eligible. Valley residents can learn about Medicare and what healthcare benefits they are entitled to through free daily presentations at the Valley Baptist Health Plans office at 2005 Ed Carey Drive in Harlingen—located right across the street from Valley Baptist Medical Center-Harlingen. Residents may make appointments for the free consultations by calling 1-877-422-4400. (TTY/TDD 800-562-5259.) More information is available on the Internet at www.valleybaptisthealthplans.com.

Valley Baptist Health Plans is one of only six health plans in Texas to receive the award for above average care of diabetes, a major health problem in the Valley. Members of Valley Baptist Health Plans can receive free diabetes testing supplies and free educational programs to help them live long and healthy lives in spite of diabetes. The award from the Texas Diabetes Council is based on performance indicators in the 2004 Guide to Texas HMO Quality, which is available online at www.dshs.state.tx.us/thcic/publications/HMOs/HMOReports.

Golden Palms Retirement and Health Center, a continuing care community, offers a spectrum of lifestyle choices for retired men and women, allowing them to enjoy living in a thriving community adjacent to VBMC-Harlingen. Golden Palms residents can participate in active, independent living in contemporary apartments, or opt for assisted living apartments and, when necessary, the twenty-four-hour skilled nursing center. The Chandelier Dining Room is open to the public for lunch and dinner.

Valley Baptist's approach to wellness and medical care is holistic, paying attention to mental, physical and spiritual needs, following the model of Jesus Christ's healing ministry. The Department of Pastoral Services trains

Above: Valley Baptist Health Plans is the Valley's only locally-owned health insurance plan, with offices at 2005 Ed Carey in Harlingen.

Below: Golden Palms Retirement and Health Center offers active, independent living in an attractive setting in Harlingen.

chaplains and offers confidential spiritual care and skilled grief and crisis counseling twenty-four hours a day. The Valley Baptist Health and Fitness Center provides a family-oriented environment for healthy exercise. The spacious new facility in the Treasure Hills Country Club offers cardio and strength training equipment, exercise and spinning studios, a multipurpose gym, and an indoor exercise pool, along with classes, trainers, and childcare.

Valley Baptist's Value Partners Program includes an Employee Assistance Program available to local employers with services including counseling by licensed mental health providers and spiritual care through a professional chaplain from Valley Baptist. EAP services help lower healthcare costs, reduce turnover, and increase productivity. Value Partners enables businesses to take part in professional development on topics such as training for supervisors and team building.

The strong and steady expansion of services of the health system has been the result of the

combination of skilled and compassionate staff, advanced medical technology, faith, and most recently, a full commitment to the continuous improvement of customer service and medical Best Practices.

"There is no greater priority for our system than continuous improvement so that we can provide the best possible outcomes for each of our patients," said James G. Springfield, FACHE, president and CEO of Valley Baptist Health System.

Valley Baptist's facilities are among the first American hospitals to apply the Six Sigma quality improvement program, maximizing both staff performance and patient satisfaction. Six Sigma initiatives are helping save lives and significantly reduce healthcare costs. The initiatives have included evidence-based medical management of heart attack, heart failure, and Coronary Artery Bypass Surgery, all resulting in better patient outcomes. The U.S. Centers for Medicare & Medicaid Services has ranked VBMC-Harlingen number one nationally in the treatment of heart failure, an accomplishment heralded in *U.S. News and World Report*. It also ranked the hospital in the top ten percent nationally in the management of acute myocardial infarction patients. Valley Baptist's quality initiatives have resulted in decreased turnaround times in the Cardiac Catheterization Laboratory and other services. VBMC-Brownsville, which received a national PRC Award for Outpatient Quality of Care, has attained dramatically improved outcomes for patients with heart attacks and heart failure. In addition, Six Sigma is addressing the prevention of adverse drug reactions, prevention of infections, and a multitude of other issues. Valley Baptist has also activated Rapid Response Teams in Brownsville and Harlingen to evaluate and stabilize critical patients. Numerous other achievements, such as streamlining the outpatient registration procedures, online and by phone, are resulting in increased customer satisfaction. Valley Baptist is committed to transparency; the public can review the organization's quality results by going to www.valleybaptisit.net and clicking on the large button entitled "Our Quality Results."

An ongoing information technology transformation at Valley Baptist saves time

and simplifies daily processes such as retrieving medical records, writing prescriptions, ordering tests, and viewing the results. The IMPPACT (Information Management for Physicians and Patient Access with Clinical Transformation) project will lead to greater patient safety and convenience, real time access to test results, and an improvement in patient access to higher quality care.

A prime tenet of Valley Baptist is education for patients and staff. VBMC-Harlingen is the primary teaching hospital for the Regional Academic Health Center of the University of Texas Health Science Center at San Antonio. At the Valley Baptist Family Practice Residency Program, new doctors combine their growing medical knowledge with a strong faith component. Valley Baptist also operates an LVN School and supports a spectrum of medical education through millions of dollars in contributions.

Educating the public is an equally vital mission. For example, Valley Baptist's stroke education effort is committed to saving lives and saving patients from permanent disability by making the public aware of the signs of stroke and the importance of going to the hospital as soon as possible.

At health fairs and at free seminars, Valley Baptist strives to raise awareness of multiple medical issues and to involve individuals in safeguarding their health and participating in wellness activities. On the website, www.valleybaptist.net, patients can find answers to topical questions, find a physician, or subscribe to a free E-Newsletter with timely health updates tailored to the topics that interest the patient. Through free and low cost screenings provided to communities by the Heart and Vascular Service Mobile Van and a mobile community outreach unit, Valley Baptist makes it easier for Valley residents to check their blood sugar level, their cholesterol levels, their blood pressure, and have additional testing performed. Additionally, support groups sponsored by VBHS reach out to those dealing with cancer, stroke and other illnesses.

Valley Baptist has grown in response to the needs of the community with guidance from a dedicated Board of Directors. Valley heart patients are benefiting from the new state-of-the-art Cardiac Catheterization Laboratories at VBMC-Brownsville and VBMC-Harlingen. VBMC-Brownsville recently expanded its radiology department and opened Brownsville's first all-digital Breast Center. An attractive state-of-the-art sixty-two-bed Children's Center at Valley Baptist-Harlingen is hailed both for its cheerful atmosphere and its superior pediatric care.

Notwithstanding all its achievements, Valley Baptist Health System is focusing on what will be accomplished in the years ahead. Its goals are no less than to implement important changes in healthcare delivery that will reduce preventable illnesses and deaths. These goals will be achieved through a commitment to relentless service, service expansion, and quality second to none.

Above: Valley Baptist Medical Center-Brownsville recently received national awards for care of stroke and heart patients.

Below: Valley Baptist Medical Center-Harlingen is the Valley's first Lead Level 3 Trauma Center and features a rooftop heliport.

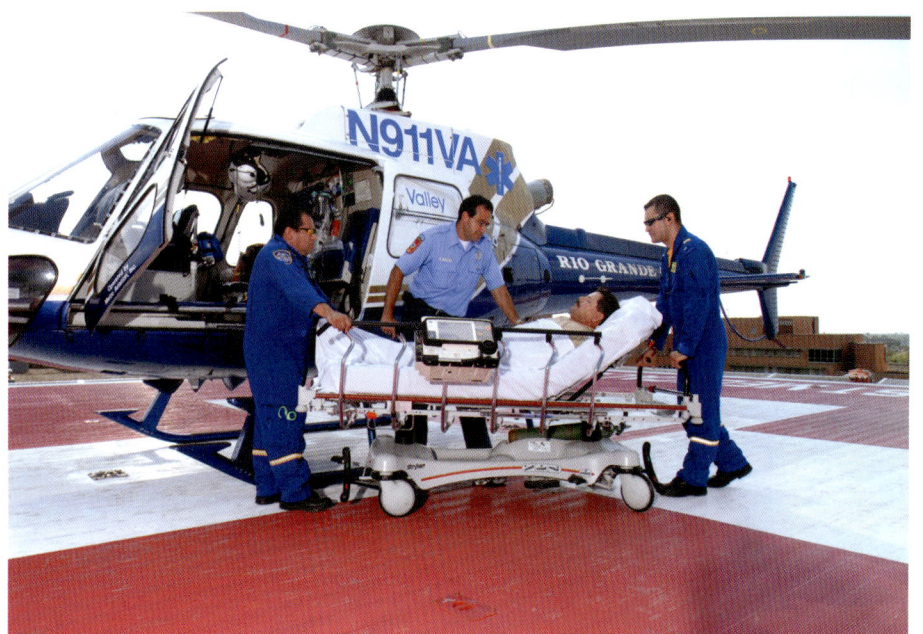

SU CLINICA FAMILIAR

Since 1971, Su Clinica Familiar has been filled with purpose, commitment and compassion; reaching out to the community in its mission to heal and comfort those individuals lacking access to basic healthcare and support services. The united effort of dedicated professionals, employees and concerned community leaders has been the foundation that has led the way in achieving a high standard of excellence in healthcare delivery and clinical education while making a difference in the lives of so many Valley residents.

With five clinic sites spanning Cameron and Willacy Counties, Su Clinica Familiar has grown to be a highly respected and vital part of the medical community. As a result of Su Clinica Familiar's strong commitment to innovation, continuous quality improvement, and patient centered care, it is poised to further strengthen its reputation as the comprehensive medical home of choice for the Rio Grande Valley.

The seed for Su Clinica Familiar was planted in the late 1960s. This seed blossomed in the 1970s with the opening of the first clinic in Raymondville and continues to grow strong and proud into the twenty-first century.

In 1971, Willacy County found itself in a healthcare crisis. The county's migrant healthcare program faced closure due to a loss of federal funding. Without support from Washington, the county's resources would be insufficient to sustain the program. County officials held out hope that a dedicated group of individuals, led by Catholic Charities, Inc. and Organizaciones Unidas, would secure government approval to operate a clinic providing preventive health and primary care.

Gaining the necessary federal funding from the United States Department of Health, Education, and Welfare (HEW), Su Clinica Familiar opened its doors on May 1, 1971 under the direction of Dan R. Hawkins, Jr. Since that day, it has continued to respond to the needs of the community while reducing the financial burdens of county and local governments.

The early years of Su Clinica Familiar were marked by a rapid expansion of programs designed to meet the needs of the community. Initially, there were two clinics, one in Harlingen to serve Cameron County and one in Raymondville to serve Willacy County. Within six months of opening it doors, Su Clinics began offering maternity services. The Medical and Nutritional Outreach program was initiated in 1972 to provide basic medical services to rural communities. The Project MANO mobile unit was also put into service to bring a "clinic" to those unable to travel. That same year, Su Clinica entered into an agreement with the National Health Service Corps to provide medical professionals to underserved areas.

During the mid-1970s to early 1980s the clinic expanded its programs and added dental services through the leadership of its Executive Director, Francisco G. Gonzalez. In May of 1980, the clinic achieved the size and stability to operate independently from the administrative support given by Catholic Charities and was incorporated as Su Clinica

Su Clinica Familiar is the medical home of choice for over twenty-five thousand residents of Cameron and Willacy Counties.

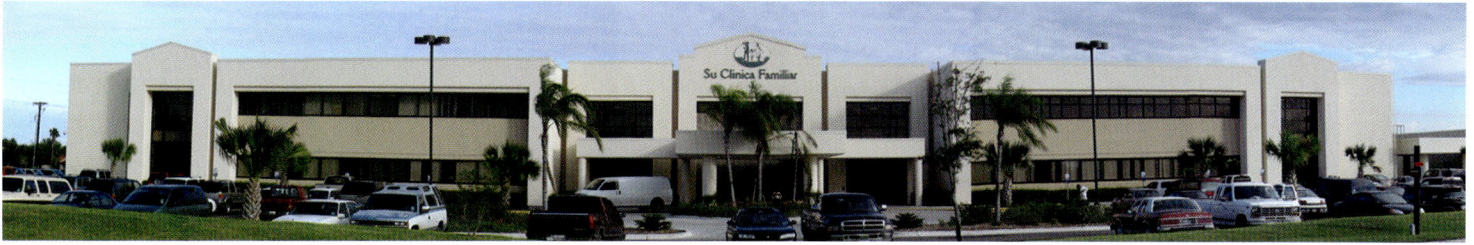

Familiar, Inc. During the tenure of Gonzalez, Su Clinica Familiar achieved recognition as one of the first migrant clinics in the nation to be accredited by the Joint Commission on the Accreditation of Healthcare Organizations (JCAHO), a standard of excellence that the clinic maintains to this day.

In 1986, Brownsville native, pharmacist, and pediatrician, Elena Marin, M.D., was hired and in 1988 assumed the position of Medical Director. In 1995 she served as Medical Director and Executive Director, and in 1996 was selected as Executive Director, ushering in a new era of visionary leadership for Su Clinica.

In 1998, Su Clinica became a key player in bringing a much-needed medical education presence to South Texas through the establishment of the University of Texas Health Science Center at San Antonio's Regional Academic Health Center (RAHC) in Harlingen. As a principal partner along with Valley Baptist Medical Center, the clinic provides medical students and residents a unique opportunity to gain frontline experience in treating many of the perplexing medical conditions prevalent along the Texas-Mexico border. Fostering a unique synergy of primary care, medical education, and hospital care, the partnership has solidified Harlingen's growing medical complex as one of the state's centers of excellence. The integration of medical education programs complements Su Clinica's longstanding commitment to providing educational opportunities for dental students and allied health professionals.

Su Clinica Familiar has always been known for the highly credentialed, caring staff of professionals who have dedicated their careers to providing health services to underserved populations. This includes caring for all people who face barriers in accessing services because they have difficulty paying for services, because they have language or cultural differences, or because there is an insufficient number of health professionals/resources available in the community.

Su Clinica's transformation from a small migrant clinic into the region's leading community health center fostered a need for a modern, new facility, which could efficiently serve the desires of the community. In 2000, serving an expanding base of over 24,000 clients with over 100,000 annual visits; Su Clinica's leadership set the goal of constructing a patient-friendly facility that would also nurture the learning experience through its affiliation with the Health Science Center Medical School.

Construction started on a new primary care, multi-specialty clinic in 2001 and the doors were opened to the clinic's patients in October 2002.

The results have been spectacular. The sixty-two-thousand-square-foot headquarters and clinic boasts four 'mini-clinics' housed under one roof, providing separate admissions and waiting areas for each of its four specialty areas: dental, women's health, pediatrics, and internal medicine.

Keeping its promise as a one-stop medical home for the entire community, Su Clinica offers: pediatrics, internal medicine, family practice, OB/GYN, minor surgery, podiatry, and pharmacy. Lab and x-ray, twenty-four-hour on-call hospital coverage, health professions training, dental services, nutrition, health education, social services, outreach, case management, integrated eligibility screening, and specialty referral coordination round out the clinic's core services. Su Clinica staff also takes pride in opening its pediatric wing weekday evenings and on Saturday and Sunday to fulfill its pledge to those who need care.

Su Clinica Familiar's multispecialty headquarters facility is located in the heart of Harlingen's medical center complex.

Building upon its steadfast commitment to promote a healthier community, Su Clinica's staff is expanding the reach of its healthcare system by going directly into the neighborhoods to provide outreach services that make a difference.

Based out of the Raymondville clinic, the Diabetes Case Management program provides an individualized, one-to-one program to monitor and treat some of South Texas' most prevalent diseases. Case managers work directly with the patient and physicians to offer counseling and advice, knowing that effective management of the disease often leads to a more fulfilling and rewarding life for the patient.

It is this extra effort and personalized attention that is also at the core of the Healthy Start program. Focused on pregnant women with special needs, Healthy Start provides face-to-face meetings with the mother-to-be, starting with prenatal care and continuing until the child reaches two years of age. Dedicated case managers engage mothers in a variety of educational training and counseling programs including parenting skills, the advantages of breastfeeding, financial tools and planning, wellness, and healthy baby programs. Strengthening ties with the public, a volunteer advisory board provides suggestions for improvement and expansion of the program.

Being one of the nation's fastest growing metropolitan areas, the Rio Grande Valley will continue to experience a high demand for quality healthcare services well into the future. Su Clinica Familiar is leading the campaign to empower our communities and create a healthy future for the next generation.

Su Clinica Familiar currently has six facilities: two in Raymondville and one each in Harlingen, Brownsville, Santa Rosa, Sebastian, and Lasara. To meet the growing needs in Brownsville and southern Cameron County, the clinic's board of directors has adopted a strategic plan to grow and expand in response to unmet needs. One of the largest employers in the area, the clinic's staff has grown from 26 employees to over 320 professional and administrative staff. In 2006 the

dedicated team of over 30 medical and dental providers and their support staff provided affordable, quality services to over 25,000 patients through more than 147,000 patient visits.

As Su Clinica Familiar moves forward towards the horizon, its future holds the promise of harnessing the vast potential of tomorrow's technology through the implementation of an electronic health records system. Together with the inauguration of behavioral health services within the primary care setting, Su Clinica Familiar is poised to strengthen its reputation as 'the medical home of choice' for the Rio Grande Valley.

Holiday Inn Express Hotel & Suites and Hometel Haciendas

Holiday Inn Express Hotel & Suites in Weslaco has been a shining star from the day it opened in 2004. In 2005 the hotel was selected as the Best New Hotel in the Holiday Inn Express Hotels and Resorts system. In 2006 it ranked among the top 20 outstanding hotels in the 2,000-strong Holiday Inn Express chain and received the 2006 Quality Excellence Award.

Holiday Inn Express guests are responsible for catapulting the locally owned and managed Weslaco hotel to the top of the charts because of their satisfaction with the total guest experience. The awards also reflect close adherence to Holiday Inn Express' high standards of hospitality and housekeeping.

The success of Holiday Inn Express in Weslaco began with choosing the right builder: Darwin Dittburner, known for building success into properties by an insistence on quality construction and a perfectionist's attention to details, all enthusiastically approved by the owners, RGV Express, Ltd. Choosing the perfect location was essential: a subtropical Texas city that prides itself on quality of life, on a site near the intersection of Expressway 83 and International Boulevard so visitors can easily connect to McAllen, Harlingen, and the RGV Premium Outlet Mall in Mercedes. With the Texas A&M University's Agriculture Research and Extension Center and the USDA's Kika de la Garza Subtropical Agricultural Research Center nearby and the Progreso International Bridge and shopping in Mexico only six miles away, the Weslaco hotel is ideally suited for both business travelers and leisure tourists.

Since January 2004 when the Holiday Inn Express welcomed its first guests at the lobby's granite reception desk, the courteous and well-trained staff has continued to extend South Texas hospitality to travelers from across the U.S. and around the world. Hanging behind the reception desk, an original Gabriel Salazar landscape offers a glimpse the region's agricultural heritage in a painting of Rio Grande Valley cotton harvesting with a backdrop of wide blue skies and palm trees edging the horizon. The lobby showcases three of Weslaco's distinctive stores—Bugambillas, Boots 'n Jeans Western Wear, Lionel's Western Wear—and gives just a hint of exhilarating shopping opportunities only minutes away.

The Great Room next to the lobby invites guests to gather informally on comfortable sofas and easy chairs to chat, enjoy the fireplace or watch the big screen television. A window wall overlooking the year round heated pool and Jacuzzi brings in tropical Texas landscaping of bougainvilleas and palms. Every morning, guests meet in the Great Room to enjoy a complimentary deluxe hot breakfast featuring omelets and true-blue Texas biscuits and gravy. The world's best cinnamon rolls, made on the spot, give every guest more than enough reason to get up and—after the first bite—have a wonderful attitude to face the day. The hotel's motto is

of the guest self-serve laundry. Local calls are free and the majority of rooms are designated as non-smoking.

The luxurious, spacious suites at Holiday Inn Express provide a full living room, desk, microwave, mini-refrigerator, and sink plus an oversize tub with marble surrounds and rain showerheads. The Queen suites feature two queen beds, and the sofa opens into a queen bed. The Jacuzzi suite with an extra-large bathroom promises relaxing hours in a luxurious private pool.

Being in the hospitality business, Holiday Inn Express recognizes that superior customer service is a fundamental part of their appeal. With a staff that is second to none in professionalism and customer care, the hotel gives guests yet another reason to love their stay in Weslaco highly and to return. For guest safety and peace of mind, a twenty-four-hour security system monitors the parking area and the entrance doors of the hotel.

Weslaco is known for its range of highly recommended restaurants, including, right next to the hotel, The Blue Onion. Famous for its Mediterranean cuisine, this restaurant has built its success on soups, salads, and

"Whatever will make you happy," and, judging by the smiles seen in the Great Room, happiness at the Holiday Inn Express is both pervasive and contagious.

Catering to the needs of business travelers, Holiday Inn Express has high-speed Internet access in all rooms, Wi-Fi throughout the facility, and a dedicated business center complete with computer, printer, copier, and fax. The hotel's two meeting rooms are configured to seat up to fifty persons for business sessions or social gatherings. Business guests and leisure travelers can take advantage of the on-site fitness center, which features two treadmills, a stationary bicycle, a stair climber, a television, of course, and the heated pool perfect for laps.

Each of the fifty-five guests rooms and forty-five suites provides travelers an attractive and tranquil haven after a busy day, whether they have come to the Rio Grande Valley on business or to enjoy a tropical adventures along the border. Equipped with a coffeemaker, iron and ironing board, and hair dryers, the comfortable, contemporarily furnished rooms are designed to make guests feel at home. Rain showerheads contribute to enhancing guests' stays. Travelers are invited to ask the reception staff for any small toiletry items that may been have forgotten at home and to take advantage homemade pizzas created with flavorful fresh ingredients. For south of the border variety, try any of the city's authentic Mexican cafes for enchiladas, tamales, and taco plates.

Weslaco's revitalized downtown of unique boutiques, antique stores and local color provides hours of shopping pleasure. The fabulous 110-store Premium Outlet Mall only minutes away can take days to explore fully. Shoppers have already discovered the convenience of making the Holiday Inn Express their home base for shopping expeditions to the outlet's Brooks Brothers, Disney, and Ann Taylor.

For a change of pace and atmosphere, guests who travel six miles directly south from the Holiday Inn Express down Highway 1015 to the Progreso International Bridge find a safe and secure two-nation mini-vacation. A twenty-five-cent pedestrian bridge toll opens up the wonders of Nuevo Progreso, a Mexican town known for pampering and entertaining the visitors who come to shop, dine and savor the flavors of Mexico. You can bring back up to $400 worth of striking pottery, silver jewelry, and Mexican curios free of import duty. American citizens will need their passport re-enter the U.S.

Nature lovers take advantage of Weslaco's fabled birding opportunities at Valley Nature Center, Estero Llano Grande State Park and Frontera Audubon Society Reserve. The Valley

is an ecotourist's heaven with over 500 bird species recorded here. Weslaco is the heart of the avian treasure trove, offering easy travel to Santa Ana National Wildlife Refuge, the Salt Lakes, and the nation's only outdoor North American Butterfly Association butterfly reserve. Weslaco invites visitors to Rendezvous with a Redhead...parrot, of course, because it is so easy to spot some of the resident wild red-crowned parrots and green parakeets. Be warned that you will hear them before you see them. Other beautiful and colorful birds include the green jay, the great kiskadee, and the very rare blue mockingbird. Dragonfly Days in May celebrate another of the city's winged treasures. Weslaco's green space includes three golf courses and city parks.

The Weslaco Airport is the Valley's private aircraft hub with twenty-four-hour services available and particularly accessible for business guests.

Holiday Inn Express Hotel & Suites is part of the InterContinental Hotels Group (IHG) and participates in the Priority Club with partners Crowne Plaza, Holiday Inn, InterContinental Hotels and Resorts, Candlewood Suites, and Staybridge Suites. Members earn points toward free nights or miles with stays at any of the facilities, and Priority Club points never expire. Priority Club has been named the Best Hotel Award Program by *Global Traveler* magazine and a consumer travel group.

Hometel Haciendas is the sister property of Weslaco's Holiday Inn Express and is located adjacent to the hotel. "Affordable luxury" is the best description of the Hometel Haciendas, which are extended stay apartments with two-

bedrooms, two-baths, each newly-furnished and fully-equipped. Conveniently located on International Boulevard, Hometel was built to exacting standards by Darwin Dittburner for RGV Express Ltd. and looks like a small, landscaped community of single-story residences.

Designed with both traveling corporate executives and retirees in mind, Hometel Haciendas present an upscale option for temporary yet long-term lodging for a week, a month or a year. Each of the twenty haciendas has cable television, phone and high-speed Internet along with individually controlled air conditioning. From the tropical lime green-upholstered rattan accents of the living room and the porcelain tile floors in the kitchen and baths to the granite kitchen counters and pewter fixtures, the haciendas radiate luxury with a tropical flair. Both bedrooms contain a king size bed. One full bath includes a Jacuzzi tub, and the second bathroom has both tub and shower. Twice a week maid service lets guests relax even more, whether inside the roomy hacienda or on their landscaped semi-private patio complete with table, chairs and a warm winter climate.

Hometel guests have full and free access to the amenities at the Holiday Inn Express, including the daily heated breakfast including those famous cinnamon rolls, the pool, laundry room, and the fitness center. Hometel

Haciendas opened in January 2006 and already residents have created a community ambiance that celebrates a pleasant place to live and a wonderful place to come home to when you cannot be at home.

Within walking distance are a number of newer Weslaco restaurants: The Blue Onion, Ron and Nancy's Little Italy and several fast food options, along with the catering headquarters for Edible Pursuits.

Several businesses share the Hometel complex's office unit: a full service barber and beauty salon named The Touch of Class, with therapeutic massage, Dr. Rock's Chiropractic office, and the South Texas School of Bartending. More information is available at www.hometelhaciendas.com.

LA JOYA
INDEPENDENT
SCHOOL
DISTRICT

La Joya Independent School District draws students from some of the Rio Grande Valley's smallest communities. In contrast, the achievements of La Joya schools and students are immense, bringing recognition and honors far beyond expectations of outsiders. The stunning success is based on the belief of La Joya educators that every student has the right to educational excellence. The school district's motto, "Engaging the hearts and minds through rigor, relevance, and relationships" expresses a heartfelt commitment to provide quality instructional programs that help students to achieve their potential and a bright future.

La Joya ISD reached a 2007 peak enrollment of 25,000 students. These students come from dozens of colonias and communities like Sullivan City, Peñitas, Palmview, and Los Ebanos, that are part of a 226 square mile area bound by the west side of Mission and the western Hidalgo County line, and reaching from the Rio Grande on the south to McCook on the north. Over ninety-nine percent of La Joya's students claim Hispanic heritage, and some of them belong to migrant worker families.

The district's thirty-two campuses encompass twenty-one elementary schools, six middle schools, and five high schools. Reflecting the fact that La Joya ISD remains one of Texas' fastest growing school districts, four of those school opened for the 2007-

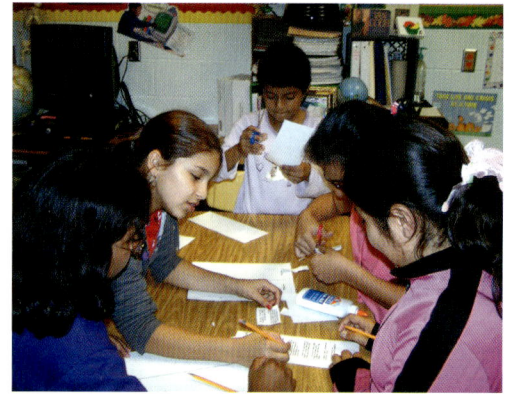

2008 school year. To teach, nurture, and challenge students, La Joya ISD employs approximately 5,000 professional and support staff.

La Joya Independent School District traces its beginnings to a small rock and adobe school built in 1849 for the children in Havana and surrounding communities. Between 1913 and 1918, two teachers at the Havana school, Nellie Leo Schunior, known as Doña Nellie, and Guadalupe Ornelas, determined that the school's mission was to provide a quality education for all youth. Schunior donated fifteen acres for a regional high school. Her vision lives on in the Nellie Schunior Middle School facility, which was dedicated in 1920 after her death.

Affirming each student's worth and promise; La Joya ISD has taken Schunior's philosophy to the next level by propounding a college-ready culture for all students, regardless of their socioeconomic and cultural status. La Joya ISD's academic initiatives have set the standard for student success through programs such as Reading Renaissance, Math Renaissance, Building Bridges, Gifted and Talented, and Bilingual/ESL. Academic excellence is nurtured through UIL, Texas Scholars, Tech Prep, Advanced Placement and Distance Learning; the quality of instruction and the engagement of active minds are evident in statistics. La Joya ISD has the highest number of students dually enrolled at South Texas College. The students are earning college credits while in high school, getting a head start on a college degree and saving money on tuition and college fees. LaJoya also has the highest number of Hispanic students in the region who score three or higher on

Advanced Placement exams for college entrance and earned a Superior Achievement rating in the Texas School Financial Integrity Rating System.

La Joya students have the unique opportunity to develop their potential both within and beyond the academic core at the Rio Grande Valley's first public school fine arts academy, the Communications, Visual Arts and Performing Arts Academy of La Joya ISD. The four-year curriculum develops students' talents through intensive arts education and performance. The La Joya Performing Arts Center showcases hundreds of performances each year by fine arts students studying music, dance, and drama. The public has responded enthusiastically to performances by La Joya ISD's renowned Mariachi "Los Coyotes," Grupo Folklorico "Tabasco", as well as presentations by the choir, orchestra, band and theatre students.

Students enrolled in La Joya's four-year Health Science Academy receive a career-based health science and technology education, customized to their plans either to pursue additional medical training or to begin working in healthcare upon graduation. In addition to challenging course work, students tour medical facilities, job shadow, and participate in community service projects that enhance their understanding of medical professions. Certification as an Electrocardiograph Technician, Pharmacy Technician, Nurse's Aid or Licensed

Vocational Nurse is available on graduation for students who complete the respective Health Science Academy programs.

La Joya ISD counts on strong partnerships with surrounding communities to help prepare all its students for success in life. La Joya offers free summer reading programs for parents. School nurses remind parents of the importance of vaccinations for their children. The seven-member School Board of Trustees connects the schools to the communities, working with school administrators to provide Pre-K to twelfth grade students with the best education possible. Board President Rita M. Garza-Uresti, Vice-president Jose A. "Fito" Salinas, Secretary Johnn Valente Alaniz along with Joe Aguilar, Arturo Gonzalez, Jr., Joel Garcia, and Esperanza Ochoa have dedicated themselves to continuing the La Joya tradition of access to quality educational opportunities for all.

La Joya ISD honors people with Community Recognition plaques for their outstanding support of education. The first honorees were Eva and Joe Maria Garza. For three generations the Garza family of Peñitas has made college graduation the expected achievement. Now the family counts thirty-two college graduates among its members.

The Superintendent of La Joya Independent School District is Dr. Alda T. Benavides, a 1971 graduate of La Joya High School, who is leading a new generation of La Joya students with vision and dedication. Dr. Benavides, who earned a Bachelor's Degree in Elementary Education and English followed by a Doctorate in Education Leadership from the University of Texas Pan American, is helping develop creative, critical thinking in La Joya students, preparing them for post-graduate success, and instilling a lifelong love of learning. Dr. Benavides holds a broad range of certifications from Superintendent and Middle Management Administrator to Counselor and Bilingual ESL.

La Joya ISD schools have been named to honor national, regional, local, and cultural luminaries. The elementary schools are Rosendo Benavides, Lloyd M. Bentsen, Jr., Enrique Camarena, Narciso Cavazos, Elodia Chapa, William J. Clinton, Eligio "Kika" de la Garza, Diaz-Villarreal, José de Escandon, Guillermo Flores, Sam Fordyce, Henry B. Gonzalez, John F. Kennedy, Leo J. Leo, Americo Paredes, Corina Peña, Patrico Perez, E. B. Reyna, Juan Seguin, Tabasco and Emiliano Zapata.

Middle schools are Cesar Chavez, Irene M. Garcia, Memorial, Ann Richards, Dr. Javier Saenz, and Lorenzo de Zavala. The older students attend La Joya Senior High School, Benito Juarez-Abraham Lincoln High School, Jimmy Carter High School, the Alternative Center for Education and Hope Academy.

La Joya Independent School District has good reasons to be proud of the students, teachers, administrators, support staff and parents. Most recently, U.S. Congressman Henry Cuellar presented a one million dollar check to La Joya ISD Board of Trustees, Administration, and staff for being the only school district in the Rio Grande Valley and one of only five in the State of Texas to receive

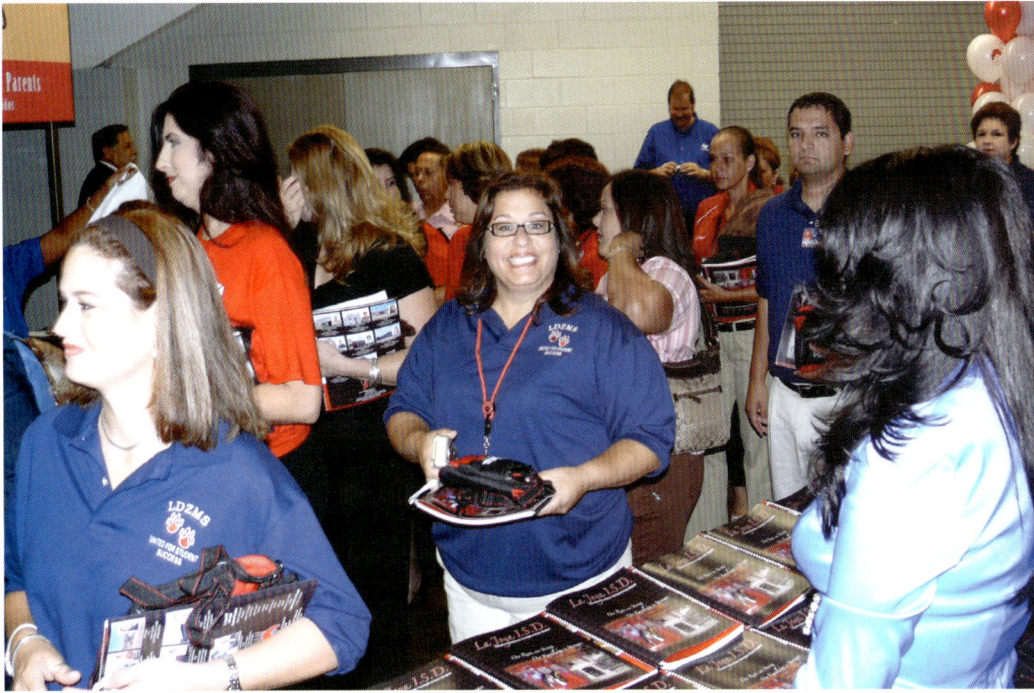

grant support from the U.S. Department of Education. These funds will be used to implement the "Passion for United States" (PUSH), a comprehensive three-year American History teacher professional development project whose primary goal is to raise student achievement in the area of traditional American History by improving the quality of instruction in kindergarten through twelfth grade traditional American History.

"Teachers participating in the PUSH will have an opportunity for sustained hands-on staff development in traditional American History, which will inspire them to inspire the students in their classrooms. This will undoubtedly improve the teaching and learning of traditional American History in La Joya ISD classrooms," says Dagoberto Ramirez, La Joya ISD Social Studies Coordinator.

Working together, La Joya ISD continues to create outstanding educational opportunities that set the stage for the future success of all students.

CITY OF WESLACO

Weslaco has it all—a thriving downtown, a quality of life for visitors and its thirty thousand residents that is second to none, and a booming business community being transformed by developments in eco-tourism, retail, logistics and manufacturing.

Located in the middle—the heart—of the dynamic Rio Grande Valley, Weslaco possesses the many elements that make an ideal city for people to live and work and play. Superior public and private schools along with excellent post-secondary educational opportunities enable individuals to keep growing along with their city.

The renovation of the fabled Cortez Hotel into the Villa de Cortez signaled Weslaco's entry into the twenty-first century. With its boutiques, second-floor ballroom, office space, and chic café, the Cortez is the centerpiece of Weslaco's ongoing downtown revival. Retailers and business professionals are discovering vibrant urban neighborhoods, both downtown and in shopping districts throughout the city.

The Weslaco Chamber of Commerce, the Weslaco Economic Development Corporation, and the Visitor Center occupy a distinctive southwest-style complex that, sited on a one-time produce packing shed lot, acknowledges the city's past while setting the standard for Weslaco's revitalization and Weslaco's future. The EDC recently launched the Heart of Weslaco program designed to

make the Texas Boulevard and Business Highway 83 region into an attractive business destination through landscaping and architectural and infrastructure upgrades. By recruiting businesses to Weslaco and aiding local businesses' expansion plans, which add well-paid jobs to the economy, the EDC helps create an even more prosperous and enjoyable city.

Leading companies are discovering that placing their headquarters in Weslaco means they can supply services and deliveries up and down the Valley with greater convenience and lower costs, thanks to a central location. FedEx Ground operates its Valley-wide distribution center from Weslaco while a delicatessen wholesaler supplies stores from Laredo to Corpus Christi from its Weslaco headquarters, and, in 2007 HEB, opens its regional distribution center in Weslaco to supply dozens of Valley stores.

The newest segment of Mid-Valley Industrial Park, a designated Foreign Trade Zone, opened in September 2006 offering facilities ready for occupancy by businesses expanding locally or relocating to the heart of the Valley. Ideal for light industry, service suppliers, and freight companies, the park is adjacent to the Weslaco Airport, which is becoming a prime base for regional corporate aircraft, attracted by its 5,000 foot lighted runway and twenty-four hour aircraft fuel

service. Weslaco is the home of the Valley's Super National Guard Armory.

Beyond being a cost-effective location with a business-friendly environment, Weslaco offers a young, educated, and available labor force. The city's three vocational and junior colleges—South Texas College's Mid-Valley Campus, South Texas Vo-Tech, and Valley Grande Institute of Academic Studies—develop young professionals through a combination of technical training and academics. South Texas College also provides customized workforce training programs for businesses.

Knapp Medical Center claims the distinction of being the city's largest private employer with a staff near 1,000, among them many healthcare graduates of the local colleges. The 233-bed hospital is a Level III Trauma facility.

Weslaco is well known for offering a slice of the good life, too. Festivals, dining, shopping, entertainment, and recreation—residents and visitors can take their pick of a menu of events and activities for kids and adults. Every April, more than 12,000 people come to the Rio Grande Valley Onion Festival to help celebrate the official Texas Vegetable and the creation of the 1015 onion in Weslaco. Onion-eating and onion-cooking contests, all-day entertainment including dancing horses, arts and crafts booths, and festival foods add up to a memorable, full day of fun for all. Tejano music energizes City Park during the fiestas of Cinco de Mayo and

Dies y Seiz de Septiembre, while the RGV Music Festival heralds four days of nearly nonstop country and bluegrass favorites every March in nearby Mercedes.

Three remarkable nature parks bring out the wild side of Weslaco. An urban refuge covering five acres, Valley Nature Center is renowned for its native plants, which attract butterflies, colorful birds such as red crowned parrots, groove billed anis, green jays, chachalacas, and humans, too. The center's educational programs on natural history and

native landscaping have introduced many to the Valley's wealth of natural resources. Frontera Audubon provides varied bird habitat, while the recently opened Estero Llano Grande State Park is the wetlands gem of the World Birding Center parks. This 176-acre refuge, which includes a segment of the Arroyo Colorado rimmed with marsh cane, is a magnet for wading birds like the wood stork and roseate spoonbill. Bird walks, nature hikes and school programs are open to the public. The city's older neighborhoods, shaded by massive live oaks, mesquites, and subtropical foliage, offer havens for flocks of wild parrots.

Among the city's recreational assets are six city parks with programs for children and adults and tennis courts. Two eighteen-hole golf courses, the acclaimed Tierra Santa Golf Club and the Mid-Valley Golf Course along with the nine-hole Executive Course, welcome golfers year-round. A pleasant way to exercise is to step out on the Weslaco Pacers Walking Trail, an official Volkssport course through historic downtown.

The former city hall has been restored to its elegant 1930's Spanish architecture and recognized as a historic Texas landmark along with the Skaggs House and the Tower Theater. The latter is a unique, charming little theater-in-the-round occupying the interior of Weslaco's original water tower. The Weslaco Museum, now under construction, will display and interpret a treasure trove of historical artifacts. Weslaco's agricultural heritage lives on in the respected Texas A&M University's Agriculture Research and Extension Center, which developed the 1015 onion and continues to make advances in agricultural production and contributing to the competitiveness of American agriculture. At the adjacent campus of USDA's Kika de la Garza Subtropical Agricultural Research Center, scientists pursue research in crop quality, integrated farming and beneficial insects while citrus research has been the focus of the Texas A&M-Kingsville Citrus Center since the 1940s. The famous Rio Red grapefruit is one product of the extensive research conducted here.

Since 1946, when the Valley's first modern travel trailer park was opened by the R. S. Parker family in a former Weslaco cotton field, Winter Texans have been welcomed into the region's fabric of life. From Weslaco's numerous recreational vehicle parks, Winter Texans contribute thousands of volunteer hours at Knapp Medical Center, the schools, in the library, and churches.

Only seven miles south of Weslaco, the Progreso International Bridge connects visitors to an easily accessible Mexican adventure. Bustling with shops, restaurants and street vendors, Weslaco's sister city Nuevo Progreso offers an exciting, no-hassle dip into a fun-filled foreign culture. A Mecca for both winter Texans and local residents, Progreso has so much to see and so many bargains that few shoppers can resist the silver jewelry, wind chimes, beach dresses and braids of garlic. Everyone settles in for an authentic Mexican plate of enchiladas, fajitas or chicken tacos with guacamole and an icy margarita. The modern bridge with canopied walkways across the Rio Grande diverts heavy traffic to separate commercial lanes.

The reputation of Weslaco's progressive business climate and supportive community is growing. But the quality of life is an even stronger attraction. That's why, more than ever, families and businesses are turning to Weslaco for their own slice of the good life.

For additional information on beautiful Weslaco, visit www.weslaco.com.

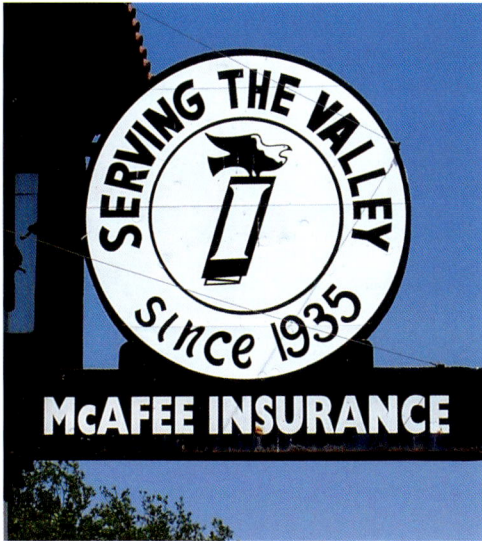

For over seventy years, "McAfee Insurance" has been a highly respected name in Mercedes, Texas. It was founded in 1935 by Richard R. McAfee, who owned and operated the agency for over thirty-five years. When Robert Garza bought the agency in the early 1970s, he retained the McAfee name, realizing it was a well-known symbol for excellent quality and dedicated service. On July 1, 1983, Murray Schlesinger joined the McAfee team and has been an integral part of the growth and success of the agency.

McAfee's mission is to provide its customers expert advice and responsive customer service while providing the most competitive pricing available in the insurance marketplace.

Today, under the leadership of Garza, now joined by sons Richard and Robert R., the agency continues to grow into a strong leader in the commercial insurance industry. Its twenty employees serve clients across the Rio Grande Valley to San Antonio. Through the expertise and dedication of its professional staff, McAfee Agency continues to specialize in the complexities of commercial insurance.

The agency has grown at a steady pace through the years, keeping up with the rapid growth of the Rio Grande Valley. It specializes in the selling and servicing of commercial insurance in the construction, trucking, and produce industries, and has been instrumental in developing insurance products for these industries. The company also specializes in hard to place property risk;

insuring a large amount of property on South Padre Island.

McAfee's group health benefits division specializes in selling and servicing large group health products to public entities. Its small commercial division specializes in assisting small businesses manage their insurance needs.

"Many of the insurance companies we represent specialize in insuring specific types of businesses or industries, offering special coverage and pricing," said Garza. "Every business and industry is unique. We identify ways to properly insure the unique hazards of a business. As business owners ourselves, we understand the special protection businesses need to prosper." The McAfee Agency, located in a landmark building near Business Highway 83 and Texas Boulevard in downtown Mercedes, is an integral part of the Rio Grande Valley business community. It is a member of American Subcontractors Association and Associated General Contractors, and is endorsed by the Texas Produce Association for their insurance needs.

The Garzas and other agency personnel are active in area Chambers of Commerce and many other civic and community organizations. For additional information on McAfee Agency, visit www.mcafeeagency.com on the Internet.

The McAfee Agency: Robert Garza, seated with sons Robert R. and Richard Garza, and partner Murray Schlesinger, who joined the agency in 1983.

MCALLEN INDEPENDENT SCHOOL DISTRICT

One hundred years ago, in 1908, the first school opened in McAllen. It was a one-room, white-framed structure that stood on the corner of Twelfth and Austin Streets.

One century ago, one teacher worked with twenty children from all grade levels. They concentrated on the fundamentals—reading, writing, arithmetic, grammar and geography. It was a much simpler time with little technology—no computers, televisions, radios, or Internet.

As more children enrolled, it soon became overcrowded. So, classes were then transferred to the church.

In 1915 the Texas Legislature passed an act establishing the McAllen Independent School District. A board of trustees convened to hire teachers, set salaries and to provide transportation for the children. A year later, the board passed a bond issue for $100,000 to construct, equip and man the first brick school building. Today, an elementary school would cost approximately $10 million.

A faculty club was added in 1919 to house female teachers and their chaperones. This was a kind of dormitory that adjoined the school. According to district documents, it was the first of its kind in the country.

It was a humble and fascinating beginning, with an inspirational mark on the world that continues today.

"There is no question—we were leaders then (early twentieth century) and we're leaders now," McAllen ISD Superintendent Yolanda Chapa said. Over the years, McAllen ISD has produced extremely successful men and women—doctors, lawyers, teachers, federal judges, and even an astronaut who has trekked into space.

"Today, we are home to state, nationally and even internationally recognized students and teachers. We have the only International Baccalaureate (extremely rigorous college-level) program south of San Antonio." Amazingly, when end-of-course exams are graded in Geneva, McAllen's students (98.4

Above: In December 2007 some of McAllen's top high school scholars held a dialogue with scholars of recent years who are now in college. The idea was to tap into the unique perspective of alumni scholars to nurture our current crop of scholars.

Below: Many graduates from McAllen's high schools consistently qualify for top-of-the-line universities throughout the nation. Each year, McAllen students produce a bevy of national and even international honors.

percent) far surpass the state (76 percent) and global (80 percent) success rates.

Last year, the acclaimed IB program expanded to include elementary and middle school students. Additional elementary school staff was hired to teach art, drama and technology to ensure that children are educated to their greatest potential.

Also, McAllen students won an impressive eighty-six top honors in three national academic programs——National Merit, National Hispanic, and Advanced Placement (AP).

In fact, McAllen ISD consistently produces the most National Merit Scholars in the entire region each year—having produced fourteen in the past five years.

This year, a total of eighty-six national academic recognitions were announced:

- 2 National AP Scholars
- 12 AP Scholars with Distinction
- 6 AP Scholars with Honor
- 40 AP Scholars
- 3 National Merit Semi Finalists
- 7 National Merit Commended Scholars
- 16 National Hispanic Scholars

Additional information on McAllen Independent School District may be found on the Internet at www.mcallenisd.org.

Above: McAllen's Michael Fossum attends a parade in his honor at his old school—Jackson Elementary in the fall of 2006. Fossum became the first native of the Rio Grande Valley to become an astronaut following a space shuttle mission in July 2006.

Below: "Before 1910, the building on the left was used as a school during the week and for church services on Sunday. Several Protestant congregations shared the facility." Sources: The Museum of South Texas and McAllen Chamber, McAllen 70th Anniversary Souvenir Edition.

McAllen, Texas.

WESLACO INDEPENDENT SCHOOL DISTRICT

For the past ten years, Weslaco Independent School District has been named as a Texas Education Agency "Recognized District." Weslaco students base this designation on eighty percent mastery of the Texas Assessment of Knowledge and Skills (TAKS) tests in math, reading, writing, science and social studies.

Located in south central Hidalgo County, about eight miles north of the Texas-Mexico border, the fifty-four square mile Weslaco ISD is bordered by the cities of Progreso, Donna, Mercedes and Edcouch/Elsa.

Weslaco city officials organized the district soon after the city's establishment in 1919. With an enrollment of 350 in its first year, 1921-22, the district had a faculty of ten and a nine member graduating class. The first official school building was completed in February 1922 and was welcomed by students and staff. The new insulated building brought comfort after a harsh winter, and the students would no longer have to borrow benches from city hall.

Weslaco ISD now serves about 16,000 students, of which 97.7 percent are Hispanic. More than 3,000 students who are classified as "migrant students" leave the district with their parents during the school year for agriculture-related work.

With a current operating budget of $120,000,000 and about 2,000 employees, WISD is one of the largest employers in the city of Weslaco. Through careful financial planning, it has grown with the student population while retaining one of the lowest tax rates in the Valley. Over 500 students graduate annually from Weslaco and Weslaco East High Schools and pursue higher education.

WISD is made up of ten elementary schools, four middle schools and three high schools. Elementary schools (grades pre-kindergarten through fifth), and middle schools (grades six through eight) lay the foundation for the district's extensive curriculum. The middle school curriculum offers more advanced courses as well as fine arts and technology courses.

Weslaco's second high school, Weslaco East, opened in 2000-01. To avoid overcrowding at Weslaco High, the new school was built to accommodate ninth and tenth grades, and in time was converted to a four-year high school. Both high schools provide an array of upper-level courses, such as advanced placement. Through concurrent enrollment, students can obtain college credit or take college courses while still in high school.

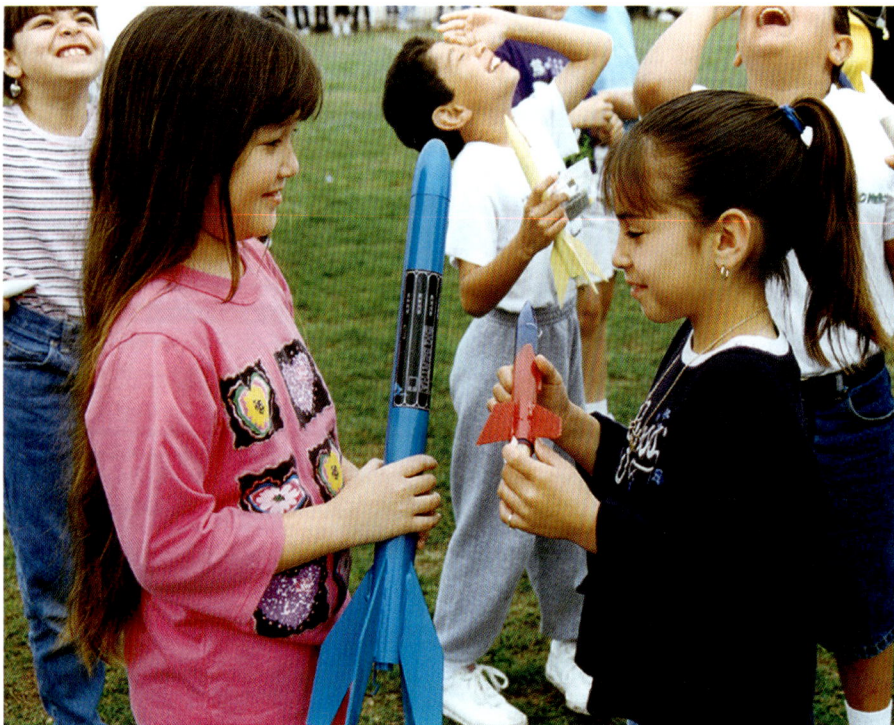

South Palm Gardens is a free-choice high school for grades tenth through twelfth. The small class size and individualized instruction offered meets the needs of students seeking a different environment from the traditional high school setting. The Weslaco ISD Guidance Center provides an alternative to suspension and gives students a second chance to improve their behavior.

All Weslaco ISD students have access to the latest educational programs and research tools, such as the Internet and a variety of software. With computers in every classroom, students are kept abreast of technological advances. Teachers utilize computers to enhance the district's tough curriculum and to track student progress through district-wide testing and grading.

Reading, writing and math skills are the building blocks that all students need to be successful. The district's eclectic approach to teaching reading includes phonics, the use of authentic literature, and integration of reading and writing. Recognizing the increasing importance of math in the age of technological advancement, WISD is committed to providing quality math education geared to each student's individual needs and abilities. Performance objectives guide teachers in planning instructional strategies to ensure continuity across grade levels.

Science and social studies concepts and skills are emphasized at all levels. At the elementary level, an interdisciplinary approach emphasizes themes that span many disciplines. At the upper levels, science and social studies become more specialized and require more in-depth learning.

Advanced Academic Services, the WISD gifted and talented program provides a quality education for all students, recognizing that each has unique needs, interests and abilities. Gifted education fosters intellectual and artistic ability, task commitment, creativity, and critical thinking. QUEST, an acronym for Questioning, Understanding, Exploring, Searching, and Thinking, is the gifted program for kindergarten through sixth grade students, which is designed to enhance education through enrichment opportunities. Key components of the secondary gifted program include the

Distinguished Achievement Plan, in which students perform at college or professional levels. This plan allows students to pursue college-level studies while in high school. Concurrent enrollment is available with the University of Texas-Pan American, allowing students to earn credit concurrently for both high school and college. The wide variety of advanced programs has earned Weslaco High School recognition as a "Mentor High School." Its advanced placement program was selected in the spring of 2000 by *Newsweek* as one of the best in the country.

The district's administration, faculty, and staff strive to provide a quality education with an innovative and challenging curriculum. Working as a team with parents and the community, Weslaco ISD will continue to ensure that all students are prepared to meet the demands of an ever-changing world.

VALLEY TELEPHONE COOPERATIVE, INC.

Top: VTX-Broadband tower San Diego, Texas. Serving Alice and surrounding areas.
PHOTOGRAPH BY ANTHONY MAZETIS.

Above: Alta Vista Subdivision. Valley's second fiber-to-the-home community.
PHOTOGRAPH BY GINA REYES.

Below: Main office located in Raymondville, Texas.

In 1952, unable to get telephone service, a group of farmers and ranchers in Willacy and Hidalgo Counties founded and incorporated Valley Telephone Cooperative, Inc. (VTCI) with a loan from the Rural Electric Administration (REA). The mission was to construct lines and establish telephone service throughout rural areas in South Texas, and the original organizers of VTCI included names long associated with the Rio Grande Valley's pioneer days: McAllen, Hester and Mayo. VTCI has carried the pioneer spirit forward by integrating its member-customers into a telecommunications network that is now global in nature. As a certified Texas telephone cooperative, VTCI is owned by those it serves—its member-customers. Further, as a nonprofit Texas telephone cooperative, by law VTCI returns any telephone-related profits over and above its operating costs to its member-customers as Capital Credits.

Headquartered in Raymondville, VTCI continues to lead the industry in bringing state-of-the-art telecommunications technologies to South Texas. From the hand-crank telephones in four original exchanges, VTCI has grown to approximately 4,950 member-customers in seventeen exchanges connected by a state-of-the-art fiber optic network traversing 7,300 square miles in nineteen counties. Today, VTCI proudly brings affordable and reliable telecommunications services second to none to its member-customers, reaching westward from Port Mansfield and San Perlita to Stillman, Lasara, Encino, Hargill, McCook and El Sauz.

VTCI provides its member-customers with a full menu of telephone services ranging from Call Waiting and Caller ID to Calling Cards and competitive long distance rates. VTCI became, in 1999, the first telephone company in Texas to become 100 percent equipped to provide high speed DSL broadband services to its members. Recently, VTCI became the first telephone company in South Texas to connect fiber optic lines directly to customer homes. Thanks to "fiber to the home" connections, the entire Rio Grande City subdivision of Country Estates and the Roma subdivision of Alta Vista have enhanced opportunities to telecommute and to obtain sophisticated distance learning and medical applications.

In 1984, VTCI entered the unregulated fiber optic cable transport business by forming subsidiary VTX Communications L.P. (VTXC) and laying a network of fiber optic cables through South and Central Texas. This fiber optic network provided connectivity for national telephone carriers to North Texas and beyond. Today, VTXC provides long haul fiber optic transport for all major U.S. and several Mexican telecommunications carriers and connects the Rio Grande Valley and Mexico to the rest of the U.S. by means of international fiber optic border crossings. High quality, affordable long distance service provided by VTX Communications is available to VTCI member-customers and to people living beyond the cooperative's regulated service areas.

In August 2001, VTCI acquired RGV Wireless, Inc. This subsidiary, renamed VTX Broadband, Inc., is the largest provider of high speed wireless Internet services in the Rio Grande Valley and a recognized leader in this industry. South Texas households that cannot get high speed broadband connections have an attractive alternative with VTX Broadband, using low profile wireless rooftop antennas.

The employees of VTCI and its subsidiaries are focused on supplying first class service to every customer—both rural and urban. One goal is to provide better service to more of South Texas by expanding the fiber optic network and adding towers in less densely populated areas.

Demonstrating its vision for the future, VTCI became one of four national beta test companies for Internet Protocol Television (IPTV). This experimental broadband service is allowing VTCI to test leading edge technology and determine the feasibility of bringing digital television to its subscribers via high speed Internet connections— thus opening up a new generation of telecommunications services. VTCI plans to leverage its technological advantages and alliances with major satellite companies to bring even more such opportunities to its member-customers.

VTCI's bond with the communities it serves is visible in the cooperative's commitment to education and economic development. VTCI is proud to award ten four-year college scholarships each year to outstanding students who reside in the VTCI service areas. VTCI further supports education by supplying fiber optic broadband connections for all five Raymondville schools as well as for all the school districts in its service areas. More than twenty years ago, VTCI began working with UT Pan Am to bring distance learning courses to rural schools. Through video connections, students are able to take classes not locally available such as advanced calculus. VTCI continues to expand educational opportunities for its member-customers, including partnering

with the University of Texas and Texas A&M systems to deliver distance learning programs. Besides being a major sponsor of STARS, VTCI, as a member of the National Telecommunications Cooperative Association (NTCA), arranges each year for a high school junior in its service areas to visit Washington D.C. to witness government in action.

VTCI's Harvey Tandem Network Operations Center in Raymondville houses the organization's main switching equipment and cable distribution frame, which is complemented by the Service Center in Lasara. In addition to its major locations in Raymondville, Lasara, Harlingen and McAllen, VTCI and its subsidiaries occupy some eighty other physical locations to serve their customers.

Above: Raymondville ISD fiber network construction.

Below: Network equipment located in the Harvey Tandem Network Operation Center in Raymondville.

BOGGUS FORD

Sixteen-year-old Lewis Boggus arrived by train in McAllen in 1917 to find his new job at the L. R. McDaniel Ford dealership involved bookkeeping and washing cars. Raised on a small ranch near Odem where he herded sheep at an early age for three dollars per month, Lewis learned to master whatever work came his way. By 1918, he was driving a demonstrator Model T around the Valley and on his way to becoming the top salesman. One day Lewis drove up behind a farmer and his three daughters who were driving a team of fine horses and followed them for nine miles to a Pharr stable yard. Lewis asked the man if had ever considered buying an automobile. The daughters, who had been trying to get him to buy a car for months, finally heard their father say he would buy one, if Lewis would teach one of the girls to drive. At that time, teaching a new car owner to drive was essential to making a sale, so Lewis readily agreed, recalling that the twenty-three year old daughter "wasn't bad looking."

Lewis sold twelve cars in his first month, combining hard work and common sense, keeping his eyes open for families with first-class horses, as they could afford a car.

At the age of twenty, Lewis bought a dealership in Mission, becoming the youngest Ford dealer in the United States. During the next few years he invested in dealerships in Raymondville, San Benito, Brownsville, Corpus Christi, Harlingen and McAllen. The Boggus family still owns operates the Harlingen and McAllen dealerships.

After graduating from Texas A&M, Lewis' son, Frank, worked in the McAllen dealership while waiting to be called in the Air Force as a Second Lieutenant due to the Korean conflict. After two years in the Air Force, Frank, with his wife Peggy and their children Barbara Sue and twins Bob and Jack, moved to Harlingen where he managed that operation. Another son, Lewis Jr., ran the Corpus Christi franchise. After Lewis' s death, Frank took over the McAllen dealership as well, building an accessible facility at a prime location along the Expressway. Frank's sons worked summers in different departments. "Never the air-conditioned ones," Bob recalls.

In 1977 when Bob graduated from the University of Texas, he went to work at the McAllen dealership and became the general manager. Jack, after graduating from Southwest Texas, was the general manager in Harlingen until his death in 1992.

Bob Boggus, who began taking over the family business from Frank in 2001, is now president of the Harlingen and McAllen dealerships. Boggus Ford is one of the top selling dealerships in the Valley. The Harlingen dealership relocated to a new,

larger, and more visible facility along the Arroyo Colorado and Expressway 83 to tap into the Valley's growing economy. With spacious showrooms to hold more vehicles, a rapid service center for oil and filter changes, and revamped service and parts departments, the Harlingen location is able to display more cars and trucks and to provide prompt service. In 2007 it became Boggus Ford Lincoln Mercury.

The Boggus Ford dealership in McAllen undergoes frequent remodeling both of the showroom and service areas to remain responsive to customers' changing needs. The addition of a quick-oil-change facility and the expansion of the pre-owned car lot have been driven by a desire to satisfy customer preferences.

Frank and Bob Boggus share a rare honor. In 1990, Frank received the *TIME* Magazine's Quality Dealer Award, the automotive dealer industry's most prestigious award, which is presented for exceptional performance and distinguished community service. Only 60 of 19,500 dealers are selected as recipients annually. In 2007, Bob received the *TIME* Magazine Quality Dealer Award, which cited his community involvement and excellence in business.

Unselfish dedication to the community is a trait Frank and Bob share. Frank was instrumental in establishing Texas State Technical College, the Boys & Girls Club, the Boggus Education Pavilion at Valley Baptist Medical Center and, with his daughter, Barbara, the Ronald McDonald House of Harlingen. He has served on and led numerous boards: Texas State Bank, Harlingen School Board, Harlingen Area Chamber of Commerce, Harlingen Rotary, Wesley United Methodist Church, Boy Scouts, Salvation Army, Texas Automobile Dealers Association, and Valley Baptist Medical Center. A leading Texas Republican, Frank is a friend of presidents and senators, as well as local and state officials.

Bob is equally involved in the community. He has led the Valley Partnership (the regional Chamber of Commerce), Texas Automobile Dealers Association, Fellowship of Christian Athletes, and the Salvation Army. He serves on the boards of Valley Baptist Medical Center, McAllen Chamber of Commerce, Texas State Bank and is a Deacon of the Baptist Temple.

Three generations of the Boggus family have helped build the Valley's economy and helped make the wheels go round. Bob and his wife, Karen, have three children, Ashley, Austin and Katie, which means a fourth generation is waiting in the wings.

CITY OF HIDALGO

More than 250 years of history and heritage are woven into the fabric that is the city of Hidalgo. Yet the illustrious past of explorers and adventurous pioneers is matched today by Hidalgo's community spirit and vision of a dynamic future.

Missionaries to the Coahuiltecan Indians established the tiny Mission San Joaquin del Monte on the north bank of the Rio Grande in 1749. Opposite present-day Reynosa, the mission was included in a 1767 Spanish land grant. When the Mexican-American War ended in 1848, John Young built a trading post on the river, naming it Edinburgh for his native town. The bustling river port soon became the county seat for Hidalgo County and in1861 changed its name to Hidalgo. The Rio Grande in flood washed the town away several times, but the residents persevered and rebuilt.

The community's prosperity was evident in the handsome border brick architecture of homes and the Hidalgo County courthouse and jail built in 1886 and in the local ferries shuttling cargo and some of Hidalgo's 400 residents to and from Reynosa. Although

Above: Borderfest.

Below: The Pump house.

political maneuvering shifted the county seat north in 1908, the region's agricultural boom was already transforming the region. Pulling hundreds of thousands of gallons from the Rio Grande, a steam-powered pump at Hidalgo began supplying irrigation water to newly cleared farmland in 1910.

A suspension bridge over the Rio Grande in 1926 strengthened the links between Hidalgo and Mexico, just as Hidalgo's current twin international bridges reinforce the cultural and economic ties between the nations. With approximately 500,000 border crossings monthly, Hidalgo is the nation's fourth largest land port of entry, welcoming millions of foreign visitors and returning Americans. The city's links to global trade remain strong due to the customs brokerages and manufacturing distribution centers located near the international bridge.

More than a mere connection to elsewhere, Hidalgo is increasingly a destination for people who love nature, history and a lively culture. The city's designation as an All American City in 2004 was due in part to its distinctive museums, festivals, and historic landmarks and in part to its residents who are rightfully proud of their community and its achievements. Hidalgo's welcoming atmosphere and its attractions have enticed thousands of winter Texans to make the border city their home away from home.

Construction of City Hall Plaza, echoing the brick architecture of a century earlier, helped launch the city's renewal in 1995. Hidalgo had already turned its notoriety as the U.S. entry point of killer bees (Africanized

honeybees) into a claim to fame with a ten-foot tall statue of the world's largest killer bee. The original irrigation district Pump house, shuttered in 1983, underwent a complete restoration and opened in 1999 as the Hidalgo Pump house Heritage and Discovery Museum. Showcasing the power of steam, the museum helps visitors picture how irrigation water changed a veritable desert into fertile farmland. The Pump house, now tucked in a cove of the Rio Grande and edged by dense native brush, also offers a habitat rich in native plants and the wildlife attracted to them and has been designated a World Birding Center satellite.

For more than thirty years, BorderFest has celebrated heritage and music during its five-day extravaganza of tropical exuberance every March. Now attracting over 65,000 people, BorderFest offers live entertainment on sixteen stages, and features the arts, crafts and music of a different ethnic heritage each year.

Since 1990 the Hidalgo Festival of Lights has awed viewers with a full month of stunning light displays and light sculptures, from the Twelve Days of Christmas to Cinderella's coach and horses. Revamped and expanded each year, the light displays are created by city employees and volunteers. For fifteen consecutive nights, free musical performances feature local choirs leading to the Festival's spectacular finale—the Ramon Ayala Posada—and the presentation of toys to 10,000 children by the Hermes Music Foundation.

The opening of Dodge Arena in 2003 heralded a major transformation of Hidalgo,

much as the Pump house had, almost 100 years earlier. As the region's premiere venue for concerts, sports, and major events, as well as the home of the professional Killer Bees Ice Hockey team, the arena is attracting development, which will include lodging, retail, and restaurants.

The city's two school districts, Hidalgo and Valley View, have won statewide recognition for the excellence of their programs and their graduates although they serve low to moderate income pupils. In addition, Hidalgo ISD's Superintendent, Dr. Daniel P. King, was named 2006 Texas Superintendent of the Year.

"So many great people are working with the city that it makes it easy for me to be mayor," says John David Franz, attorney and Hidalgo five-term mayor. Hidalgo may be a small community, but it is bursting with community pride and spirit....with good reason.

Above: Dodge Arena.

Below: Festival of Lights.

RIO FARMS INC.

Above: Blanc du Bois grapes.

Below: Mr. and Mrs. Verle Crick and children outside their Rio Farms house in 1954, their last year as tenant farmers. Crick went on to lease 960 irrigated acres in west Texas where he put into practice the techniques acquired at Rio Farms.

Deep in the Great Depression, W. A. Canon, a Farm Security Administration employee, realized that the assistance provided to low-income farmers involved too much red tape and governmental interference. He proposed that local situations could best be handled on the local level by the FSA loaning money to a nonprofit farm corporation, which would then aid the sharecroppers.

Chartered by the State of Texas as a nonprofit Charitable and Benevolent Institution of Applied Agriculture on December 8, 1941, Rio Farms, Inc. opened with a $1.3 million loan from FSA and a goal of assisting low-income farmers in the Rio Grande Valley. The original board of directors, four FSA employees and three Valley residents, purchased 26,000 acres in Willacy and Hidalgo Counties to service their charter purpose. That board then resigned to make way for local citizens interested in the problems faced by low-income farm families.

Rio Farms knew their venture was successful when they were able to repay the fifty-year $1.3 million FSA loan by 1945, just four short years after the funding of the loan. Free of government obligations, Rio Farms then focused on its founding principles: helping small, low-income farmers by training them to farm successfully, to apply for agricultural benefits, to market their products, and to meet their social concerns. Each tenant family could stay on the 80 to 120 acres of Rio Farms land assigned to them for up to five years while they learned efficient farming methods. By saving their earnings, the families would be prepared to move onto a farm of their own.

Some of the Valley's most productive farmers of the 1940-1960 eras got their start at Rio Farms' as tenant-trainees. During Rio Farms first fifty-five years, over 1,000 tenants received invaluable on-the-farm-education with Rio Farms and then moved on to operate farms or businesses of their own.

Responding to changing needs and changing times, in 1972 Rio Farms changed its basic philosophy and reincorporated as an Agricultural Research and Demonstration institution, a 501c5.

In the more than thirty years since that transformation, Rio Farms has fulfilled its goals as a private research foundation. Working in conjunction with the Texas A&M Research Center, the USDA-ARS, and many researchers in private industry, Rio Farms has conducted experiments to enhance regional agricultural productivity. Its work continues to complement but not duplicate federal and state efforts to improve and expand the agricultural horizons of Valley farmers with new crops and new cultivation and irrigation methods. Rio Farms has participated in testing alternative crops such as kenaf, soybeans, grapes and tobacco suitable for the subtropics, while other experiments test new varieties of cotton, sugar cane, and grain sorghum.

The farm's efforts have often centered on improving the citrus industry through rootstock and variety evaluations. The citrus block adjacent to Rio Farms dates from the 1950s and is a testament to a joint effort of the farm and the USDA to determine the most viable and productive rootstock. The Swingle citrumelo rootstock is a product of that effort and is still one of the most popular rootstocks used today world wide. The citrus industry in Texas, Florida and California uses the results of that research to this day. Seventy percent of the Valley's sugar cane acreage is planted in

varieties studied and demonstrated at Rio Farms with agreements in place with Texas A&M to co-release future varieties for local production. Rio Farms has approximately five acres of vineyard, studying production and viability of disease-resistant grape varieties for wine production. The Black Spanish and Blanc Du Bois varieties have shown both good production and characteristics of quality wines, while being resistant to Pierce's Disease.

Several soybean varieties with juvenile characteristics and a line of pink eye southern peas were bred for maximum adaptation to Valley conditions and have been grown successfully for many years here.

Demonstration work is an important, on-going part of every grain sorghum, cotton and corn growing season. Rio Farms field days and field trials are much anticipated events that give both growers and the industry the opportunity to view varieties, fertilization and irrigation methods.

Rio Farm's fourteen current tenant farmers are raising crops on approximately 16,000 acres. The income that Rio Farms receives is used to pay taxes as well as to maintain the farm and to support the research staff that conducts demonstrations and research on nearly 1,200 acres. The sharecrop income also funds industry research projects.

With no owners and no stockholders, Rio Farms qualifies for the label unique. Rio Farms is directed by a board of five local industry leaders who contribute their expertise, experience and insights. Jesse Russell of Progresso is Board chairman; Jack Harbison, Jr., is vice chairman; and N.H. "Happy" Kitayama of Donna is secretary/treasurer. Other directors are Sam Sparks of Santa Rosa and Danny Butler of Raymondville. Jim Lauderdale provides his services to the Board as General Counsel. Dale Murden is Rio Farms' general manager and president of the Corporation, while Andy Scott, is Director of Research.

With their guidance and efforts, Rio Farms adheres to its sole purpose: public benefit and service to agriculture, evolving to meet the needs of the farming industry.

Above: Rio Farms' 1948 field day and summer legume demonstration on cow peas attracted farmers interested in improving production of the crop.

City of Mercedes

A dynamic city at the geographic center of the Rio Grande Valley, Mercedes continues to attract new residents and visitors. With a commitment to a high quality of life and a pro-business mindset, Mercedes' 15,000 plus residents share a pride in the heritage of their 100-year-old city. They share, too, a positive vision of Mercedes' future and are working with their city leaders to achieve the goal of being the preferred destination for travelers from Mexico and Texas, as well as establishing the city as a wonderful place to raise a family and start a business.

Originally part of the 1790 Llano Grande Spanish land grant, the Mercedes community arose in 1904 when developers began preparing rich delta land for farming. Incorporated and given the name Mercedes in 1907, the community thrived as an agricultural hub, with corn, citrus, and cotton being grown locally. Railroad cars filled with fresh vegetables pulled out of the city's depot throughout the winter.

Mercedes' success comes from building on its best asset, its residents. Mercedes' teachers, civil servants, businesses, and community all collaborate on building a better community for their children by focusing on education. Education has long been a critical component of Mercedes' strength. Mercedes features two public school districts and two private schools. Mercedes is home to two of the region's most prestigious specialized high schools: South Texas School for the Health

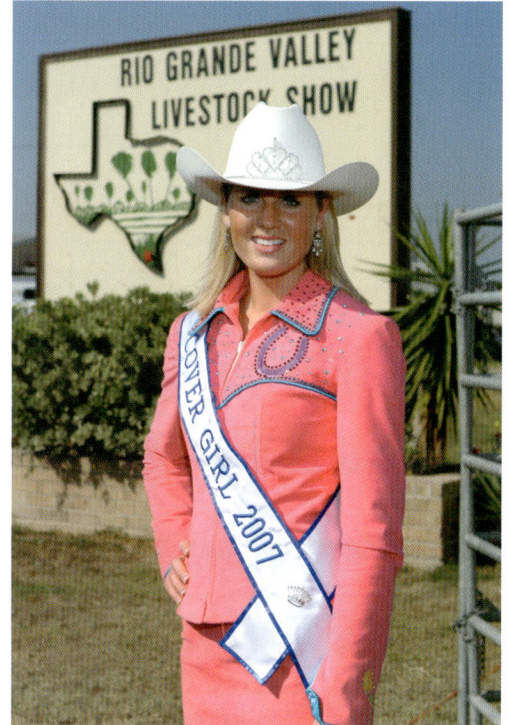

Professions, known as Med High, and the School for Math and Sciences, Sci Tech. Receiving national recognition, Med High was ranked by *Newsweek* magazine to be one of the top hundred high schools in the United States. Annually, ninety-four percent of Med High graduates enter college. Mercedes Independent School district has a total of ten campuses. The two faith-based private schools focus on elementary education.

While looking to the future, the city takes pride in looking back to its farming heritage. The Rio Grande Valley Livestock Show and Rodeo is one of the state's largest livestock shows and rodeos and has been held in Mercedes since 1939. The annual livestock celebration of youth and agriculture attracts over 250,000 visitors during the show's ten days and nights. It is jam-packed with concerts, entertainment, 4H and FFA members showing lambs and Santa Gertrudis cattle, and rodeo events. This venue, located in north Mercedes, hosts numerous events throughout the year including the South Texas Music Festival, the Smokin' of the Rio Texas State Barbeque Cook-Off, an RV Show and a Boat Show.

Downtown Mercedes continues to be the center of local business. The downtown area has long been known for its small town

hospitality, yet it offers all the services needed by the local shopper. The city's industrial zones provide attractive sites for manufacturing due to its geographically centered location in the Rio Grande Valley and its easy access to international ports of entry and major highways. Rios of Mercedes continues to craft handmade boots for dignitaries, celebrities and working cowboys. The motivated boot buyer can fly a private plane into a nearby airfield that gives easy access to shops, recreation programs at city parks, and golfing at two distinctive eighteen-hole golf courses landscaped with lush topical foliage. The Palms at Mid-Valley offers eighteen holes of challenging fairways lined with over 1,000 palm trees, while Llano Grande Golf Course is one of the oldest courses in Texas. It is a historic par seventy-two golf course that was built in 1925 yet is well-maintained and still challenging today. It is also part of a large and growing Winter Texan haven known as Llano Grande Lake Park Resort and Country Club.

At the start of the twenty-first century, Mercedes began another startling transformation. The Rio Grand Valley Premium Outlets, a $68 million, sixty-acre development, opened in Mercedes in November 2006 with over 100 stores and changed how Valley tourists shop. The tremendous success of the mall also changed Mercedes into a year-round shopping destination as thousands of people from north and south of the border flocked to buy hard-to-find, high quality merchandise at affordable prices. Premium stores finding success in this outlet include Banana Republic, Calvin Klein, Nike, Ann Taylor, Coach, Burberry, Sony, and dozens more. Plans to expand the outlet mall are underway and will add to the diversity and unique characteristics of Mercedes' shopping experience.

Pharr-Reynosa International Bridge

One of the most important ports of entry on the U.S.-Mexico border, the Pharr-Reynosa International Bridge is the only commercial bridge crossing in Hidalgo County. With over 2,155,000 crossings annually, or an average of 176,600 commercial and passenger vehicles per month, Pharr Bridge ranks as the fourth busiest crossing on the South Texas border. No other bridge crosses as much vegetables and fruits.

While the Pharr Bridge connects Mexico's fastest growing city, Reynosa, Tamaulipas, to the city of Pharr, which is part of the rapidly-growing McAllen Metropolitan Statistical Area, at the same time the international bridge funnels traffic from the Rio Grande Valley and across the United States to Reynosa and nearby industrial parks, to Monterrey, to Matamoros and beyond. The Reynosa International Airport is only five miles from the bridge. Because it makes Mexico easily accessible for commercial and leisure traffic, the Pharr Bridge area has attracted increasing numbers of trucking companies, warehouses, custom brokerages, warehouses and support services. Now located at the center of an international logistics and distribution hub, the Pharr Bridge provides four crossing lanes that contribute to its reputation for speedy international crossings. Four additional lanes are ready for expansion.

When the Pharr-Reynosa International Bridge opened in 1994, it signaled the end of

a thirty year-long quest by the city of Pharr. Building the bridge required the coordination of U.S. and Mexican federal and state agencies, along with permits from the International Boundary and Water Commission, Texas Department of Transportation, Natural Resources Conservation Commission, Texas Parks and Wildlife, and many more.

The Pharr-Reynosa International Bridge is considered the longest stand-alone international bridge in the world, with a span that stretches for 3.2 miles over the Rio Grande, which at that point is less than one-tenth of a mile wide. That long span reflects an environmentally sensitive design that protects an essential wildlife corridor along the Rio Grande. The Pharr Bridge is renowned as the most ecologically sound of all the international bridges on the Mexico-U.S. border because it has directed so much effort to preserve critical habitat for native animals, birds, and plants. In addition, when the river is at flood stage, the Pharr Bridge by design offers the least possible barriers to water flow, both safeguarding the structure and giving the Rio Grande more space within the levees.

Vehicles arriving from Mexico at the Pharr Bridge's U.S. Border Inspection Station are greeted by fifteen large butterfly sculptures. The Milagros Migrando/Migrating Miracles were created by Alison Sky in 1998 to represent both the human traffic that flows back and forth over the bridge and the diverse wildlife that sees no barrier between the neighboring countries.

Through the butterflies, the artist emphasizes the importance of metamorphosis, the transformation from a humble caterpillar to a beautiful creation. America's pre-Columbian cultures often used the butterfly as a symbol of

rebirth and spiritual transformation. Sky stated that mutual respect and collaboration between cultures and ecosystem represents the future of our planet. On a small scale, fragile butterflies are intimately connected to the natural environment, and so represent interdependency. A close look at the aluminum and glass butterflies, modeled on the Monarch butterflies that migrate between Mexico and United States, reveals that the wing patterns are composed of images of human eyes.

Mexican travelers refer to the Pharr-Reynosa International Bridge as 'the Intelligent Bridge' because of its state-of-the art technology that includes GAMMA Ray inspection equipment and programs such as Free And Secure Trade (F.A.S.T.) and ACE. With the expedited inspection of documents and cargos under these programs, Pharr Bridge has earned the reputation as the bridge with the shortest crossing times. Importers, exporters, domestic and multinational manufacturing companies find a competitive advantage in using the bridge. The strategic location at the start of Mexico's road system, the bridge's surrounding infrastructure and services along with the potential for growth combine to create an optimized experience for businesses.

The U.S. Border Inspection Station at the Pharr Bridge includes four passenger inspection stations, dedicated truck booths, and docking areas that are able to handle fifty trucks at a time. Because of the rapid fast crossing time for commercial trucks, the cold storage area for perishables is rarely called into service. The station houses the Texas Alcoholic Beverage Commission, city and county law enforcement, bridge administration office, and the USDA.

The Pharr Bridge is administered by a five member Bridge Board who determine the policies in the best interests of the bridge and the city of Pharr. Jesse J. Medina, former Police Chief of Pharr, is the Bridge Director, supervising a staff which includes thirteen toll collectors. The Pharr Bridge is open from six o'clock in the morning to midnight every day.

Construction in Mexico will soon enable traffic from U.S. 281 to cross at the Pharr International Bridge, pass through Reynosa, and travel to San Fernando and Ciudad Victoria via the International Trade corridor.

NRS Consulting Engineers

In 1984, Joseph W. "Bill" Norris arrived in Harlingen for what was supposed to be a twenty-four month engineering assignment. Twenty-four years later, NRS Consulting Engineers are the go-to guys for award-winning solutions to pressing water needs in the Lower Rio Grande Valley.

"One opportunity lead to another," says Bill, "and that two years stretched into two-plus decades."

A lot happened along the way. In 1988, Bill established NRS Consulting Engineers. In 1991, Jesús Leal joined the firm, becoming a partner in 1997. Together, Bill and Jesús developed a team of top-notch professionals, making NRS Consulting Engineers a name synonymous for innovation and expertise in water engineering. In 2008, NRS is celebrating twenty years of engineering better communities.

Under the leadership of Bill and Jesús, NRS has assembled a toolkit of cutting edge strategies and technologies for maximizing available water supplies.

"At NRS, we think outside the box," says Jesús. "And we've found that our clients value the fresh approach we bring to identifying and developing alternate water supplies."

Those clients encompass the full range of water users in the Valley—municipalities, irrigation districts, public and private water suppliers, industrial users—as well as regional entities charged with water resource planning.

The results have set the bar for water engineering, not just in South Texas but across the Lone Star State. Thanks to NRS expertise, the Valley can boast of several "firsts" that couple fundamentals of sound engineering with creative problem-solving. Several of these have been honored with awards from state and national organizations, including the WateReuse Association, Texas

NRS principals Jesús Leal and Bill Norris.

Section-American Water Works Association, and National League of Cities. They include:

- The first seawater desalination project in Texas. NRS designed, constructed, and is managing the state's first seawater desalination pilot plant. The project, conducted for Brownsville Public Utilities Board with major funding from the Texas Water Development Board, is the next step toward building a full-scale facility capable of harnessing the Gulf of Mexico as an alternative, drought-proof source of water for the Lower Rio Grande Valley. The plant will be sized to initially produce up to 25 million gallons per day (MGD) of water.

- NRS also is conducting a similar pilot for the Laguna Madre Water District. The pilot will test the feasibility of constructing a 1 MGD reverse osmosis plant to meet peak demands on South Padre Island, where the population increases five-fold during spring holidays and summer vacations. According to NRS analyses, building a seawater plant to meet peak demand is more economical than expanding existing plants or building new conventional treatment facilities.

- The largest regional network of brackish groundwater desalination facilities in Texas. NRS has designed and constructed a network of reverse osmosis plants to serve customers of North Alamo Water Supply Corporation in rural areas of Cameron, Hidalgo, and Willacy Counties. The Lasara Treatment Plant, the first to come on-line, in January 2005, is producing 1.25 MGD of drinking water. The plant has been designed so that its capacity can be doubled as the region grows. The price tag for drilling wells and constructing the new RO plant in Raymondville is less than what North Alamo WSC would have spent just on surface water rights for a new conventional treatment plant. Owassa and Doolittle plants are under construction with a total capacity of 7.0 MGD.

- NRS also provided engineering, project management, and construction services for a 2.25 MGD reverse osmosis plant to treat brackish groundwater. The North Cameron Regional Water Project, completed in 2007, serves customers of North Alamo WSC, East Rio Hondo WSC, and the City of Primera.

- Previously, NRS planned, designed, and managed construction of a 7.5 MGD brackish groundwater desalination plant, then the largest of its kind in Texas. The Southmost Regional Water Authority's reverse osmosis plant serves multiple municipal entities in south Texas. This alternative water supply provides more than forty percent of the annual needs of each entity, thus decreasing the area's dependency on the over-allocated Rio Grande. The plant, which began operating in spring 2004, is delivering "bottle quality" water at standard treatment costs of about $1.80 per 1,000 gallons.

- First NADBank-funded agricultural water conservation project in the U.S. NRS managed the first water conservation project completed with funding from the North American Development Bank. The U.S. Bureau of Reclamation provided additional funding. The project, undertaken for Cameron County Irrigation District No. 2, was part of a suite of infrastructure improvements that are saving almost 12,000 acre-feet of water per year: more than 3.6 billion gallons of water.

- The improvements included replacing a hundred-year-old pumping station, engineering a new canal interconnect and over seventeen miles of canal lining, and converting open canals to underground piping. The projects came in $2.2 million under budget and six months ahead of schedule, largely because of NRS project management strategies.

- NRS also managed installation of a package of new automated metering technologies from Australia that are saving an additional 9,000 acre-feet of water per year for the district. The technology, the first of its kind in Texas, combines flow meters with wireless operations and remote monitoring to control vertical gates and thus promote operating efficiencies.

- The first desalination plant in the Valley. NRS handled pilot testing, permitting, design, and construction management services for the first municipal reverse osmosis treatment

plant in the Lower Rio Grande Valley, operated by Valley Municipal Utility District 1. The plant, constructed in 2000, produces 250,000 gallons per day of drinking water from brackish groundwater.

- The first direct wastewater reuse facility in Texas. NRS designed and served as project managers for the Harlingen Wastewater Recovery and Reuse Facility, which used reverse osmosis to treat wastewater for direct reuse as a high quality water supply for a Fruit of the Loom factory. The facility, completed in 1990, was the first of its kind in Texas and the largest direct reuse of wastewater treated by reverse osmosis for high quality industrial purposes. NRS services included planning, permitting, design, construction management, inspection, facility start-up, and personnel training. The company also has conducted studies evaluating the potential for reuse for a number of other service providers in the Valley.

"Reuse, desalination, and conservation are just a few of the water development strategies in the NRS toolkit," Bill notes. "We are committed, as residents of the Valley, to putting all of them to work to ensure adequate supplies of safe, reliable drinking water for the next generations to come."

For more information on NRS, log on to www.nrsengineers.com.

An array of reverse osmosis membranes at North Cameron Regional Water Project.

MR. G
PROPANE

Few people observing fourteen-year-old migrant worker Amador Garcia with his family in the fields of Texas and California could have guessed at the success he would make of his life. Amador, who became the well-known and well-respected "Mr. G," was born on February 9, 1946 in Ciudad Mier in Tamaulipas, just across the border from Roma, Texas, Starr County, into a financially-deprived family. He moved to Roma with his parents and seven siblings in 1962. Years of hard labor as a migrant worker motivated Amador to continue his education. He graduated from Roma High School in 1966, the first in his family to earn a diploma. Drafted into the United States Army during the Vietnam War, Amador served in Korea. On returning stateside, he became a U.S. citizen and married Noemi Villarreal in 1970, Noemi had already begun her teaching career immediately after graduating from college in 1969.

The young couple moved to Dallas where Amador worked several part-time jobs while attending college at East Texas State (now Texas A&M at Commerce) under a Veterans Administration program. Prior to receiving his Bachelors of Science in Education, he held a part-time management job at "Mr. M Food Store" where he originated the concept of Mr. G. Jobs and college classes were not the only demands on his time; so were the additions to his family. Omar Garcia was born in 1972 and Zinnia Iola in 1974. After graduating in 1974,

In Loving Memory...
Amador "Mr. G" Garcia
1946-2002

Amador began teaching physical education at the elementary and junior high levels and enrolled in classes for a master's degree. Yet his dream was to become an entrepreneur.

Amador Garcia's opportunity to make the dream a reality occurred in early 1979, when he and Noemi relocated to the Rio Grande Valley to be closer to their families.

The first few months were a struggle for the Garcia family. Noemi continued to teach while Amador pursued his dream to have his own business. Always a devoted father, Amador would take his young daughter with him on his quest. Then in April 1979, he found a McAllen convenience store on North Tenth Street that needed a new owner. He knew he had found his calling and named the business Mr. G Food Store. Three years later, he purchased property in Mission on North Conway with an established business on site which he also called Mr. G Food Store.

While running both convenience stores, other business opportunities arose. A family friend suggested entering the propane industry and, following a short-lived partnership, Mr. G Propane opened for business as his first cylinder-filling station.

Amador saw the immense possibilities of the propane industry and being a self-starter, he immersed himself in learning the propane business, going to Austin for safety training,

Above: "Mr. G," Amador Garcia.

Below: Mr. G's grandkids: Zadriana Elizondo, Nicholas Garcia, Alexis Garcia, and Avery Garcia, 2007.

studied the industry rules and regulations mandated by Texas Railroad Commission, and received his ownership certificate. Always willing to take on more, Amador decided to expand the business in 1990 and purchased a bobtail delivery truck. With his one man operation, he serviced the entire Valley while cold calling from Brownsville to Encino and Roma. As demand from his customers increased, Amador realized the company's potential for growth. What he had begun as an on-site cylinder-filling station was maturing into a strong and prosperous business, a business that would be a legacy for his children to carry on.

Within a few years Amador acquired several small propane companies that he knew would benefit from being part of a well-organized family owned business. Amador understood the importance of keeping and satisfying customers by offering a variety of propane products and services. Because of his plan to increase the company's product line, the client base grew to include residential, farm and commercial accounts such as adult day care facilities, manufacturing plants, dry cleaning firms, sports arenas, restaurants, produce warehouses and other retail establishments. Thousands throughout the

Rio Grande Valley now recognize the name Mr. G and can thank him for providing them with access to exceptional service and a full array of propane parts and products

Unfortunately, devastation struck the Garcia family in September 2002 when Amador, the beloved Mr. G, passed away suddenly of a heart attack. But, inspired by his dedication, hard work and vision of the American dream, the family and Mr. G employees carry on steadily with the Mr. G Propane business.

Amador's wife and children are grateful for the gift of his love and his visions for a brighter future.

Above: A Bobtail truck in memory of Mr. G., 2007.

Below: The Mr. G family: Eddie Elizondo, Zinnia Garcia Elizondo, Noemi Garcia, and Omar Garcia, 2007.

City of Edinburg Chamber & Edinburg EDC

Above: The Hidalgo County Courthouse.

The spirit of Edinburg is best characterized by an event in the 1950s when the city known as the Gateway to the Valley had no hotel. Residents decided the best way to get a hotel was to invest in a community corporation, which would build a first-class hotel. Hundreds of people pooled their money, and the Echo Motor Hotel became reality in 1959. Today it is one of twelve hotels in the city. Because of ongoing and innovative collaborations like that between city government, local businesses and residents, Edinburg has three times been named an All-America City; 1968, 1995 and 2000.

A settlement named Chapin at a wide spot on a South Texas cattle trail became the Hidalgo County seat in 1908, and three years later the community changed its name to Edinburg. By 1915, Edinburg's economy was shifting from ranching to agriculture and trade. Since then oil and gas, manufacturing, and education have spurred the city's growth to more than 62,000.

Long a preferred residential community, Edinburg is evolving into an educational, research and technology center. One of the city's greatest resources and economic drivers is the University of Texas Pan American, now 17,000 students strong. The growth of Edinburg, in fact, parallels the development of post-secondary educational opportunities in the city. Edinburg

College was established in 1927, the year Southern Pacific trains first came to the town's new depot. Shortly after Grandview Hospital opened and the Chamber of Commerce was chartered in 1932, the school became Edinburg Junior College. In the 1950s, as the city built the Echo Hotel, Pan American College became a four year school. In 1989, the institution became part of the University of Texas system. With fifty-six bachelor degree programs, forty-five masters and two doctoral programs, UTPA has earned a reputation for producing top notch science and engineering graduates as well as winning the top ranking for graduating the most Hispanics with degrees in education. With UTPA's combination of bright young minds and seasoned mature intellects, Edinburg boasts a dynamic cultural scene extending to art, music, dance, and drama and lecture series. Adjacent to the campus, the Regional Academic Health Center houses the medical research facility of UTHSCSA. Cooperation between the university and the city is evident, for example, in their joint use of the popular $5 million Edinburg Baseball Stadium.

Edinburg Consolidated Independent School District educates and motivates 30,000 students, in one of the state's largest districts which covers 945 square miles. The city hosts a regional magnet school for Business, Education and Technology known as BETA Academy.

Since 1990, the Edinburg Economic Development Corporation has stimulated business activity by assisting existing businesses in expansion plans and by attracting new businesses. The EEDC laid the foundation for growth by acquiring land and putting in infrastructure suitable for light manufacturing and service industries. Edinburg's three industrial parks represent economic diversification in response to the global economy. Park tenants are primarily component manufacturers and logistics service providers for major industries with maquiladora operations.

In a recent six year period, the EEDC supported ninety-nine projects that generated about $417 million in private investments and created 6,600 jobs. Edinburg International Airport in the Foreign Trade Zone is undergoing a multimillion dollar expansion to better meet the needs of general aviation and cargo carriers.

Additionally, Edinburg's strong health services sector is attracting educated, highly-skilled employees to the new Doctors Hospital at Renaissance and to the expansion of Edinburg Regional Medical Center.

The Edinburg Chamber of Commerce, housed in the restored Southern Pacific Depot with the EEDC, has grown to represent 600 businesses, offering members networking and educational opportunities through Leadership Edinburg, Edinburg Expo and a Public Affairs luncheon. A volunteer-based organization, the Chamber organizes community events such as Fiesta Edinburg, which draws over 10,000 to its February parade and entertainment. On Independence Day weekend, the Chamber's Texas Cook'em-High Steaks attracts 100 cooks for $15,000 in prizes for the best steaks, chicken brisket and ribs. December brings the Night of Lights celebration.

The Museum of South Texas History, or MOST-History, offers a world-class perspective of the region from prehistoric indigenous people and conquistadores to pioneering ranching families and traders. Among its multiple recreational facilities, the city has three golf courses—Los Lagos Golf Club, Monte Cristo Golf Course, and the Ebony Hills Golf Course—that take advantage of the semi-tropical climate. Edinburg Municipal Park shares its site with the Edinburg World Birding Center, a beautiful native habitat known for its butterfly gardens, dragonfly pond and the colorful waterfowl

drawn to the reservoir. The Edinburg Baseball Stadium provides first-class entertainment for the entire Valley.

As the County Seat, Edinburg is the home of a busy County Courthouse, Hidalgo County administrative agency, and numerous legal offices.

In Edinburg, 100 years after its founding, vigorous growth is presenting its own challenges. The City and EDC are addressing those challenges head-on with a Master Plan that enables the city to promote orderly development through phased infrastructure projects involving drainage, roads, and schools.

While welcoming what the future will bring, Edinburg respects its past.

Above: The Museum of South Texas History.

MAGIC VALLEY ELECTRIC COOPERATIVE, INC.

In the 1930s, Rio Grande Valley towns were booming, thanks to the bounty of citrus, vegetables, and cotton produced on the fertile lands. However, the farmers and ranchers responsible for producing the crops were being left in the dark with no electricity. The existing power companies declined to run electric lines to far-flung farmhouses, forcing rural residents to rely on ice boxes, kerosene lamps, and gasoline engines.

In September 1937 a group of Valley farmers decided it was time to take advantage of the 1935 Rural Electrification Act (REA), created by President Franklin D. Roosevelt. Magic Valley Electric Cooperative, Inc. (MVEC) was chartered, adopting the region's nickname that celebrated the rich farmland on which farmers could raise two and three crops a year. With a $200,000 loan, Magic Valley Co-op began the construction of south Texas' first rural electric lines. Within a year, power was traveling through seventy-five miles of line to 125 rural homes.

The first Board of Directors reflected the widespread demand for rural power lines: George C. Darnell of Mission, R.M. King of Harlingen, L.H. Henry of Mercedes, V.W. Bernard of Edcouch, Robert Ray of Lyford, B.K. Moncrief of Edinburg, and G.W. McCain of San Benito. Early on, MVEC set a standard of fiscal responsibility that endures: the first infrastructure loan was repaid fourteen years ahead of schedule.

Its consumers, the residents of Cameron, Hidalgo, Willacy, Starr, and Kenedy Counties, own MVEC. Co-op members have a voice and a vote in electing MVEC's Board of Directors. As a nonprofit organization, MVEC is committed to supplying energy at cost to its members.

In the early 1960s, MVEC began issuing checks for Capital Credit, sending Magic Valley members their portion of the co-op's income that exceeded operating and capital costs. MVEC was the first electrical co-op in the United States to adopt Capital Credit refunds, but it has now become standard practice nationwide. "Magic Valley's management team makes decisions based on the needs of its members, not on profitability," says Chairman of the Board, Dr. Martin Garcia. "Like private utilities, we use the power of customer-members to buy electricity and equipment at the best possible price. Unlike them, we pass our savings on to our members."

Beginning in 1975, MVEC received certification from the Texas Public Utility Commission to provide service in all areas where its lines extended. Rural acres were being transformed into subdivisions, malls, schools, and logistics centers. As the Valley changed, MVEC's commitment never changed. It continued its mission of improving energy reliability while providing members with the lowest energy costs possible.

After power was deregulated, Magic Valley Co-op signed a wholesale power contract with Calpine Energy Services, which operates two generating facilities in northwest Edinburg. Recognized as one of the world's most

competitive energy producers, Calpine uses highly efficient modern equipment to produce cleaner, more reliable energy. MVEC has also joined the generation and transmission cooperative known as South Texas Electric Cooperative to foster price stability while diversifying its fuel supply. In the future, by tapping into STEC power, which is generated by a variety of sources including natural gas, lignite coal, and hydro, MVEC will benefit both from alternative fuel sources and economies of scale.

Today MVEC serves areas in and around the towns of Alamo, Brownsville, Combes, Donna, Edinburgh, Harlingen, and the list goes on. The Co-op's 4,373 miles of energized lines serves more than 86,000 meters belonging to 70,000 plus members. MVEC adds approximately 350 new members monthly. Its competitive pricing—the average 2006 residential rate was below ten cents per kilowatt-hour—makes MVEC a desirable utility provider, particularly when combined with its reputation for good service.

Providing local solutions to local questions and concerns, MVEC's 235 employees include engineers, operation superintendents, consumer service representatives and technicians who have a vested interest in the Valley communities where they live and work. Striving for greater efficiency and customer service, MVEC became the first co-op in Texas to use two-way radios in its service trucks. It continues to lead the way in safety and service, providing ongoing training for its entire valued staff.

MVEC's Board of Directors brings years of experience and commitment to their stewardship: Dr. Garcia, board member since 1972, Elton Key (1967), Frank Burns (1969), M.G. Dyer (1981), Renaldo Lopez (1992), Barbara Miller (2000), and Doug Martin (2001). They have overseen MVEC's growth into the third-largest electric distribution co-op in Texas with an investment topping $226 million.

In January 2002 the southwest style headquarters building in Mercedes was completed enabling MVEC to better manage supplying energy to an increasing number of customers in five counties. Divisional offices in Brownsville, Edinburg, and Pharr are augmented by ninety-one convenient payment centers located throughout the seven MVEC districts.

In 2007, Magic Valley Electric Cooperative, a recognized leader among cooperatives, celebrates seventy years of powering the people of the Valley.

BALLENGER CONSTRUCTION COMPANY

In 1937, with agriculture in the Rio Grande Valley booming, Joe G. Ballenger saw an opportunity. He founded Ballenger Construction Company and began constructing irrigation canals and digging drainage ditches that crisscrossed the fertile delta land green with vegetables, grain and citrus. Given the company's equipment, an expansion into land clearing naturally followed in the 1940s and 1950s. Coinciding with the national emphasis on developing major highways, Ballenger Construction in the 1960s branched into state highway construction and began taking contracts for city streets and Farm to Market roads. During the next twenty years, the San Benito-based business expanded into yet another aspect of construction and built or reworked runways and taxiways of the Valley's airports in Brownsville, Harlingen, Weslaco and McAllen. During the 1980s and 1990s, Ballenger played an instrumental role in building and upgrading the region's state highways. Around this time, the company began manufacturing hot asphaltic pavement. Soon afterward it also ventured into recycling concrete rubble and asphalt.

With the start of the twenty-first century, Ballenger moved into freeway construction and bridge building. To support and supply those activities, Ballenger acquired a caliche quarry in Hidalgo County and also began importing limestone from Mexico. The company soon purchased an asphalt cold-planing machine that grinds up old asphalt without using heat. An in-house testing laboratory was formed to monitor quality control. Because of the volume of concrete that Ballenger Construction needed to fulfill its road contracts, in 2006 it launched Tejas Concrete Company.

For sixty years, Ballenger Construction has continued to build on its successes and take the next logical steps in growing the family-owned company while building roads all over the Valley, from Roma to Brownsville to Falfurrias. Today the third and fourth generations of the family run the company. Cousins W. T. (Tom) Ballenger, Jr., and Joe Charles, Sr., and fourth generation Joe Charles, Jr., follow in the footsteps of founder Joe G. Ballenger and his sons, W.T., Sr., (Bill) and Joe Davis.

Competition drove Ballenger's expansion, yet so did a practical approach. "The more things you use, the more you do yourself," says Tom Ballenger. What comes out of the garden, goes back into the garden, he explains, revealing Ballenger Construction's long-held and much practiced recycling philosophy.

Every Ballenger project is identifiable by two Ballenger hallmarks: the quality of the workmanship and timely completion. The saying, "The road to success is always under construction" might have been created expressly for Ballenger Construction. The adage applies both to the way the company continues to seek new and better ways to build highways and to acknowledge its participation in constructing so many of the Valley's thoroughfares. As road builders with a workforce of three hundred, the company sees the bright side of road construction. But Ballenger knows not everyone appreciates the growing pains associated with road construction. The company takes its responsibilities seriously, doing whatever possible to limit disruptions for the traveling public. In fact, Ballenger has earned a reputation as a well-run company, which finishes road projects well ahead of the target date.

Ballenger Construction services extend to storm water drainage and fresh water storage lagoons, from bridge building to bridge demolition, and to pre-cast concrete traffic barriers. With some of the company's heavy construction projects valued at up to $50 million, family members are on the job every day.

The Ballenger family roots in the Valley go deep and wide. Ballengers have contributed their time and service as directors on the boards of Valley Partnership, Valley Baptist Foundation, and the Gladys Porter Zoo. They actively participate in the Texas Asphalt Paving Association and the Highway Heavy division of the Associated General Contractors of America.

MOBILE CRANE SERVICE

Mobile Crane says, "OUR BUSINESS IS PICKIN' UP!" This down-home phrase that is found on Mobile Crane Services' business cards and company literature is indicative of its friendly, honest approach to its customers but belies the knowledge and care required to successfully operate a large crane service. Lifting extremely heavy objects up in the air and then setting them down in the right spot seems simple enough but as President Jim Shawn says "Every job is different and a new challenge to do it safely and correctly." Mobile Crane Service, with over thirty-five years of experience, has met and conquered many such challenges through the years.

The company was established in 1970; on the same five-acre spot it now occupies at 807 East Business 83 in Pharr, by Shawn and five other partners who thought there might be a need for a truck crane service in the area. They purchased one crane and their first job was placing an air conditioning unit on top of the Edinburg Courthouse for TexAir Company of McAllen. Jim's brother Gene, having experience operating winch trucks in the welding, machine shop, and truck repair business he and Jim ran, was the first crane operator. The partners continued running their own businesses but found themselves buying their second crane in six months and their third crane only three months after that. The oil field business quickly became the backbone of the company, bringing rapid growth during the oil boom and remaining the largest portion of the current business mix. Oil fields require cranes to rig up and rig down drilling rigs, pump jacks, storage vessels, cracking towers, etc.

Mobile Crane's current business involves five distinct areas. The petroleum industry is their largest client base. Agriculture utilizes cranes for erecting grain elevators, cotton gins, drop legs and changing out defective equipment on these facilities. Utility companies need transformers set, towers erected and power plant turnarounds. Construction work involves erecting steel buildings, tilt wall construction and placing air conditioning units, etc. Mobile Crane services the transportation industry in highway construction, clearing highway accidents and train derailments. A relatively new but growing business is the import/export field where cranes are called upon to transfer manufacturing equipment for the maquila industry and loading/unloading large construction equipment.

The business grew so much in ten years that two of the original partners shut down their other businesses and concentrated on mobile truck crane service. The current fleet of equipment includes 11 cranes ranging in size from 18 to 210 tons, the latter being the largest crane available in the Rio Grande Valley. The company utilizes hydraulic truck cranes in its fleet. Hydraulic cranes are completely self-contained and can be driven by the operator to the jobsite and go to work almost immediately. Mobile Crane Service employs thirty-two people, including operators, riggers, shop maintenance and repair facilities, a full-time safety department, an inspection department, and office staff. The company serves customers within a 250-mile radius of Pharr, 24 hours a day, seven days a week. When a customer calls, a trained employee goes to the site to give a free job analysis, making determinations on crane size, number of men required and a jobsite inspection.

Employees of Mobile Crane Service are trained by the company and attend major monthly safety meetings as well as jobsite safety meetings prior to commencing work on any job. The key to a successful lift is a careful, methodical sequence of moves, planned in advance. Safety training is Mobile Cranes major business practice and is also necessary to meet annual safety audits conducted to satisfy the requirements of the major oil and construction companies. These audits cover safety practices, record keeping, and equipment certification. The company's motto is "FOCUS ON SAFETY, NOT THE BOTTOM LINE." Mobile Crane Service is a member of the National Crane Operators Association and Specialized Carriers and Rigging Association.

Mobile Crane has military veterans in its employment and is proud to participate in events honoring veterans at major patriotic ceremonies and events. They have purchased

a huge twenty-five by fourty-five foot American flag for hoisting on one of their cranes to help celebrate such occasions. If you are ever in the Pharr, San Juan area, please visit our Liberty Park located on Business Highway 83 as you enter San Juan from the west. Liberty Park boasts the tallest flagpole in South Texas, flying a twenty-five by forty-five foot American flag and flags from each branch of the service honoring all veterans and the armed services.

The growing economy of the Rio Grande Valley, coupled with Mobile Crane Service's professionalism, indicat that the company's business will continue to be "PICKIN' UP" in the future.

FOOD BANK OF THE RIO GRANDE VALLEY, INC.

The Food Bank of the Rio Grande Valley, Inc. started in 1983 at the Trinity Episcopal Church food pantry in Pharr. Food banks are warehouses that collect and distribute food to neighborhood food pantries, homeless shelters and soup kitchens. It was started by the Reverend Alfred "Ted" Knies and his wife, Martha, who wanted to help field workers, laborers (those who depend on agriculture to make a living) hit hard with no citrus, no jobs and no food after a freeze.

The Food Bank RGV is a distributor of donated food products from individuals, corporations and suppliers. It is the supply point for millions of pounds of food annually. As a qualified 501(c)3 nonprofit that collects, sorts, packs and distributes food to over two hundred food relief agencies in Cameron, Willacy, Hidalgo, and Starr Counties (from Brownsville to Roma). The Food Bank RGV has also accepted the challenge to help the South Texas Food Bank in Laredo become an independent organization. Therefore, in essence, it helps eleven counties.

The Food Bank RGV works on a referral system. When someone calls the Food Bank RGV for help, that person is referred to the nearest hunger relief agency in their neighborhood.

Currently, there is a staff of thirty-five people not including dedicated volunteers (some who have been there for twenty-plus years). Amazingly, it is still a grassroots nonprofit: meaning no big budgets. It is not government owned, run or operated, which means FBRGV depends on the community to survive. Ninety-eight percent of all donated monies go directly to hunger relief.

Hunger relief is the main objective but FBRGV has other programs, including Kids Cafes (after-school hot meal program), Healthy Living

(nutrition information for lower-income individuals), and School Tools (school supply assistance to teachers with low-income students).

In Fiscal Year 2005, the Food Bank RGV distributed over 21.2 million pounds of donated food and grocery products including fresh produce through member agencies consisting of food pantries, shelters, on-site feeding centers, and Kids Cafe Programs. Individuals were served over 1,300,934 times in FY 2005.

In the future, the Food Bank will call the Valley Fruit and Vegetable Company, a well known Valley landmark, home. The fourteen-acre complex anchored by a 1947 produce packing shed, got an official nod in the form of a $290,000 Preserve America award during a Washington, D.C., ceremony, one of the largest received by a city in Texas. First Lady and Honorary Chair of Preserve America Laura Bush presided over the presentation of the first round of Preserve America Grants on March 9, 2006.

The Valley Fruit and Vegetable Company building in Pharr's historic Main Street district will benefit from the funds that will go to the creation of the Farm-to-Market Museum Del Rio Grande, "a fitting tribute" to the agricultural industry of the Rio Grande Valley. To make this happen, in 2005, the Food Bank RGV initiated a

$5 million Capital Campaign. Contributing partners for this venture include: Valley cities like Pharr, Mercedes, Alton, Port Isabel, corporations like H-E-B, Texas State Bank, IBC Bank, Lone Star National Bank, foundations like the Meadows, Swalm, Loring Cook, and Mabee Foundation, McDonalds, and locals like Boggus Ford, citizens groups like the McAllen North Rotary Club and students and art faculty from the Universities of Texas Pan American and Brownsville (UTB/TSC).

Above: The Valley Fruit and Vegetable Company building in Pharr will house Food Bank RGV operations, programs and a museum.

Below: First Christian Church in McAllen is one of over 200 emergency relief organizations that are supplied with food by the Food Bank RGV.

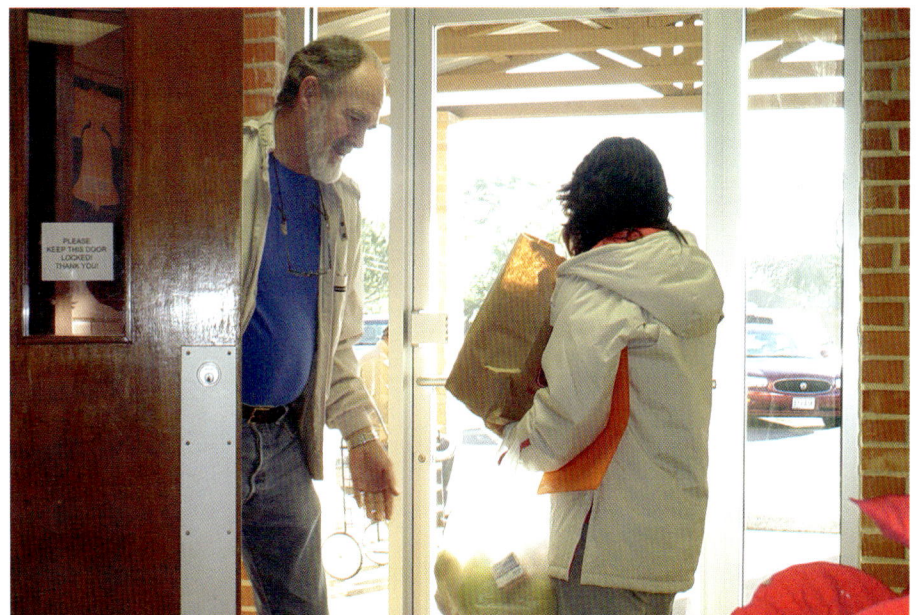

Amaida Machine Shop

After journeyman machinist Samuel Torres had managed other people's machine shops and even helped set up a new machine shop in Hidalgo, he decided it was time to apply his knowledge and skills to open Amaida Machine Shop with his wife Norma. Amaida, named for the couple's daughters Amaris and Idalia, ranks among the most technologically advanced manufacturing machine shops in south Texas.

Norma and Samuel Torres.

The 5,000 square foot Edinburg facility is equipped with precision fabrication and milling machinery that enables the company to supply custom, high-tolerance components and parts for the production equipment used by manufacturers such as Weyerhaeuser, Hi Tech Plastics and International Paper Company in the Valley and northern Mexico. On-site AutoCAD enables Amaida to download customers' engineering drawings or to create their own drawings.

Amaida is the only machine shop in the Valley that offers water jet machining. The company's massive high tech machine uses a jet of computer-controlled high pressure water to cut any type of material: aluminum stainless, brass, steel and glass as well as stone and plastics. The equipment is able to handle four by eight foot sheets of material.

Quality equipment operated by a highly skilled crew of Amaida machinists results in quality shafts, sprockets and custom parts.

Because of its attention to top quality, delivering every piece just as the customer specified and on time, Amaida is a growing business. Fast turn-around on orders is another point of pride at Amaida. When customers call with emergency requests to manufacture a critical component necessary to prevent a shut down of a production line, Amaida takes the request as seriously as the customer does, committing machinery and staff to the time-crunch challenge.

To keep up with customer demand to supply the ultimate in machining tolerance, Amaida Machine Shop plans to add a CNC (Computer Numerically Controlled) mill and lathe. For other customers, for whom parts tolerance is less critical, Amaida is bringing in a plasma cutter to provide them with a cost-effective option. To make it easier for customers to access Amaida's services, the company established a website at www.amaidamachineshop.com.

Amaida provides laser engraving on granite for memorial stones, monuments, and murals. Photographs and other images can also be engraved.

Thousands of business and leisure travelers travel to south Texas to enjoy the red-hot business climate or the semi-tropical weather. Guests' expectations of quality hotels led B & G Hospitality to begin offering deluxe hotel rooms at affordable prices in Hidalgo County. In the past two years, B & G has expanded to four well-located, three star hotels to better serve visitors to McAllen, Edinburg and Pharr.

Catering to business travelers and oil field employees, Mexican tourists and American nature watchers, B & G Hospitality specializes in hotels large enough to provide guests with the amenities they expect, but small enough to pay attention to their preferences. The properties include Country Hearth Inn & Suites in Pharr/McAllen, La Copa Inn in McAllen, and Comfort Inns in McAllen and Edinburg.

Called the "Best Value in the Valley," Country Hearth Inn & Suites combines the charm of a Bed & Breakfast with the comforts of a hotel and the security of interior corridors. Conveniently located near the intersection of Expressway 83 and Highway 281, Country Hearth offers seventy affordable rooms including twenty-seven two-room suites with privacy doors and ten hot tub king suites. Known for its Inncredible breakfasts, the hotel provides a heated pool and spa opened twenty-four hours a day. A conference room makes it easy to work away from the office. The warm and friendly staff put out fresh cookies for guests in the evening. For the convenience of our guests, an adjacent Mexican restaurant offers room service seven days a week. The hotel's night security ensures a peaceful sleep.

With all new rooms, La Copa Inn, formerly La Plaza Hotel, is very near La Plaza Mall, an extremely popular shopping destination. Free broadband Internet in all rooms makes life on the road easier for the busy business person. Guests get their day off to a good start with the complimentary hot breakfast at La Casa del Taco, a top Mexican restaurant.

B & G Hospitality's Comfort Inns feature kid-friendly suites and secure interior corridors. Each guest room offers a microwave, mini-fridge, and free high speed Internet, both WiFi and wired, among its amenities. Besides an outdoor heated pool and Jacuzzi, each inn provides a fitness center. Comfort Inns have two meeting rooms suitable for small to mid-size groups. From the Comfort Sunshine breakfast of fresh waffles to the business center and Comfort Inn's upgraded bedding, B & G Hospitality strives to make guests feel at home, far from home, according to Kamaldeep Gill, owner of B & G Hospitality.

TEXAS STATE TECHNICAL COLLEGE

Progress toward upgrading the state's technical workforce is a forty year old tradition at Texas State Technical College Harlingen.

College President Dr. J. Gilbert Leal, who is in his twenty-eighth year at the helm, led TSTC from its early mission as a vocational school to a nationally recognized technical college in mechatronics, computer gaming and simulation, medical and dental technology, and other programs that add up to more than thirty career fields with Associate of Applied Science degrees and Certificates of Completion.

"Our alliances with companies, our highly qualified faculty, our state-of-the-art facilities, and our quest for education excellence place TSTC at the forefront of the state's economic resources," Dr. Leal said.

Besides technical divisions in Computer Information Systems, Allied Health and Industrial/Manufacturing Technology, the college offers an academic core with a package of forty-eight credits transferable to any four-year public university in Texas.

Computer-aided Drafting & Design Technology student Christopher James Balli, recently crowned as Mr. TSTC 2007, is the descendant of early settlers in the Rio Grande Valley. He graduated from Donna High School in 2004.

"The TSTC instructors are very helpful. They get to know students and that motivates students to succeed," Balli said.

Building projects under way include adding lecture rooms, another laboratory and more offices for the Eddie Lucio Health Science Technology Building and expanding the Automotive Technology Building with a new laboratory for diesel engines. A new Cultural Arts Center for large events and exhibits will be built at the corner of North Loop 499 and Twenty-Ninth Street.

Some of the college's achievements in recent years include an agreement of understanding with officials from Fuzhou, Fijian province, People's Republic of China, to explore mutual interests; completion of a broader articulation agreement with the University of Texas-Pan American in Edinburg for the credit transfers of students pursuing bachelor's degrees, and an excellent accreditation ranking from the Southern Association of Colleges and Schools.

TSTC Harlingen, with an enrollment of 4,500, is part of the TSTC System. Other campuses include TSTC Marshall, TSTC Waco, and TSTC West Texas at Abilene, Breckenridge, Brownwood and Sweetwater.

The college is a two-year higher education institution emphasizing courses of study in technical education for which there is a demand within the state of Texas. For more information online go to www.harlingen.tstc.edu or call the College Information Office at 800.852.8784, ext. 4117 or 956.364.4117.

At the southernmost tip of Texas, the Port of Brownsville is a deepwater seaport serving worldwide shipping and, as the western terminus of the Gulf Intracoastal Waterway, serving barge traffic traveling the U.S. Inland Waterway System.

The Port of Brownsville, which opened in 1936, sits at the end of the seventeen-mile-long, forty-two-foot deep Brownsville Ship Channel which connects to the Gulf of Mexico at the Brazos Santiago Pass. Recognized as a major industrial center, the Port is home to over 250 companies—from an offshore oil drilling rig builder and ship dismantlers to manufacturers and petroleum storage firms—that operate within its 48,000 acres. Governed by the Brownsville Navigation District and its Board of Commissioners, the business-friendly Port of Brownsville has extensive cargo facilities including eleven deep draft dry cargo docks and one barge dock, all serviced by rail connections, and five deep draft liquid cargo docks. Ten sizable transit warehouses along with transit shed space are adjacent to vessel berths with aprons and overhead cranes. Railcar and truck loading racks at the various terminals allow safe and rapid transfer of product destined for U.S. and Mexican markets. Because the Port considers safe, secure and efficient movement and storage of cargo paramount, Port security monitors operations round the clock. Additional public warehousing is located nearby.

The Port of Brownsville is unique in offering customers five modes of transportation to and from the Port. Besides ocean going vessels, the choices are U.S. and Mexican truck transportation, rail service, barge service, pipeline access service, and air service at the Brownsville/South Padre Island International Airport.

Terminal facilities at the Port of Brownsville routinely handle and store dry and liquid bulk cargos. Commodities transiting the Port include clays, edible oils, steel, bulk minerals, fertilizers, aluminum, and chemicals. The Port's public grain storage/elevator company has the flexibility to unload and load both ships and barges.

The Port of Brownsville facilitates the movement of goods between Mexico and the United States. It operates Foreign Trade Zone Sixty-Two on more than 2,000 acres of port property and is ideally situated to support maquiladora production. Foreign and domestic merchandise can be stored or assembled in the Zone without duties being paid.

The Port of Brownsville follows a policy of well planned industrial growth and development, as demonstrated by the new Dock Fifteen and two adjoining warehouses. Not too far in the future the Port envisions expanding existing container operations and creating a second turning basin with additional docking facilities.

PHOTOGRAPHS COURTESY OF BND ARCHIVES.

Valley International Airport

In 1941, Harlingen Air Force Base was busy training air gunneries for World War II. Over twenty years later the property was declared a surplus. In 1967 the City of Harlingen took over the facility and established what is now, Valley International Airport, (VIA). Today VIA is serviced daily by Southwest Airlines and Continental Express. They offer an average of fourteen daily departures to Houston, serving both Hobby Airport (Southwest Airlines) and George Bush Intercontinental Airport (Continental Airlines). In addition, Southwest Airlines offers daily nonstop departures to San Antonio, Austin and over ten thru-flight departures to Dallas Love Field. Sun Country Airlines offers nonstop departures to Minneapolis/St. Paul between November and April. This year marks Sun Country's tenth anniversary of serving the Valley.

Strategically located in the central area of the Rio Grande Valley, VIA is the largest airport in the region and the NAFTA cargo hub for the Valley. Every year between 800,000 and 900,000 passengers arrive and depart the airport. The airport also features an international arrivals building, parallel runways allowing for simultaneous commercial operations, plenty of land for expansion, Business Class lounge, an area for children to play, restaurants, shops, and much more.

For those seeking to take flying lessons or wishing to charter their own private plane, Gulf Aviation is located in the general aviation section of the airport with its own private road and parking area.

Today, Valley International Airport and its business tenants reflect approximately 600 jobs, which provides a direct economic output estimated at over $33.4 million to the local community. The airport also provides several community-based services and programs to enhance the health, safety, welfare and quality of life of area citizens.

For additional information on the Valley International Airport, visit www.flythevalley.com on the Internet.

HESS AIR, INC.

Luis Hess was twenty-six years old and fresh from a four-year term in the U.S. Air Force when he and wife Rosemary decided to start their own air conditioning and heating business. That was thirty-one years ago. Today, Hess Air, Inc. employs a dedicated team of forty-five persons to serve their customers. The business operates from a sixty-eight-hundred-square-foot main office in Alamo, Texas, providing residential and commercial HVAC services throughout the Rio Grande Valley, as well as air filtration distribution in Monterrey, Mexico.

Hess Air, Inc. is one of the oldest air conditioning/heating companies in South Texas, and remains privately and locally owned. Satisfied customers drive the success of the business.

"Rosemary and I built this company with a commitment to excellence and a dedication to providing the best service available," Hess said. "We are proud of our team members and proud of the service we provide. But most of all, we are proud of our many repeat customers." Hess noted that some customers have been with him since the beginning—for thirty-one years— and many families are into the third generation of trusting Hess Air for their comfort.

What creates such loyalty? Hess believes it is his promise of one hundred percent customer satisfaction. "Regardless of when our customers call, they talk to real people—twenty-four hours a day, seven days a week. The technicians we send to their homes are drug free, criminal background checked, honest, courteous, and are experts at the services they provide."

What changes does Hess see in the future? "A greater focus on indoor air quality. Today's homes are energy efficient and airtight," Hess said, "and more people are suffering with asthma and allergy related illnesses."

He explained, "In this type of sealed environment, everyday pollutants such as hair sprays, air fresheners, pesticides, and other household products can't escape. Those trapped chemicals eventually make breathing difficult. We have products and services which address these problems and can help people enjoy an energy efficient yet healthy home."

Hess Air performs indoor air quality surveys and specialized air duct cleaning or replacement. Other services range from service/repair calls to replacement of existing cooling/heating equipment to sales and installation of custom-designed systems, both new and existing residential and commercial construction.

"We also repair equipment not installed by us, and often honor another product's factory limited warranty," Hess said.

Luis and Rosemary Hess are strong supporters of community and social programs of the Rio Grande Valley. Please visit Hess Air online at www.hessair.com.

Top: Luis and Rosemary Hess.

Below, Left: Hess Air in the beginning.

Below, Right: Hess Air now.

BARRERA'S SUPPLY COMPANY, INC.

Above: Barrera's Garage & Supply Company Inc., c. 1930.

Below: Barrera's Supply Company, Inc., 2002.

In the middle of the second decade of the twentieth century, Barrera's Garage & Supply Company was established at the corner of 500 North Conway in Mission, Texas. The year 1918 is the historical date used to designate BSCI's inception. Since that time, the "supply company" has provided home building materials, hardware, automotive aftermarket supplies and most recently, industrial hydraulic and pneumatic components. Sam and Ben Olivarez are the third generation of the Barrera family to manage the business.

Through the years, the Rio Grande Valley has been transformed from a rural economy to one based on urban growth—including industrial maquilas, medical centers, and retirement, entertainment, and recreational opportunities. Barrera's Supply has stayed flexible and been able to change along with the Valley's industrial needs, whether it be agricultural, automotive, hardware or industrial. During its first thirty years, Barrera's Supply Company Inc. (BSCI) concentrated in home and hardware supplies, however, during World War II, the war effort consumed much of the transportation industry's output. Once peacetime arrived, the demand for automotive aftermarket supplies increased and Barrera's Supply Co. filled that need. As non-agricultural industry began to establish itself on both sides of the Rio Grande, maintenance, repair and operational (MRO) components were needed to keep the original equipment manufacturers on schedule and BSCI again shifted its focus to meet demand.

Fluid power components are a subset of mechanical power and BSCI made the effort to shift its inventory to supply pressure hose assemblies, adapters and tubing. Meanwhile, since industrial automation uses the lighter form of fluid power known as pneumatics, a source for compressed air components was needed. Again, BSCI expanded its expertise to not only supply these, but also to supply the knowledge and training required to properly apply their use.

During the last thirty years, Barrera's Supply Company incorporated its structure and gradually gave up its stock of automotive supplies and the hardware stock shifted from the consumer to the industrial standard. In order to provide support for these components, design and application engineering functions were added to the business repertoire. Air logic and other types of control systems have been designed for many well known global customers that purchase products from BSCI.

Although the scope of products has changed, BSCI is still in the supply business and it is the ability to be flexible that has allowed Barrera's Supply Company Inc. to now provide the fluid power goods and services in demand by the industrial, construction and manufacturing businesses in the Rio Grande Valley.

Located in the Rio Grande Valley deep in South Texas, Barbee Neuhaus Implement Company has been serving the needs of a very diverse agricultural market for over fifty years. From cotton and sorghum, to soybeans and sugarcane, to vegetables and melons, they offer a full line of John Deere Agricultural, Lawn and Garden products.

They also offer other equipment lines to complement their John Deere products to give customers a choice. They have parts and service that go along with all of their products, as well as the friendly and knowledgeable people that stand behind them.

The firm began as Clifford Implement Company in 1939 in downtown Weslaco and became Barbee Neuhaus in 1974 with partners Joe Barbee and Earl Neuhaus. In 1976 the company moved to its thirty-acre location on Expressway 83 in Weslaco. Since 1996, Neuhaus and his sons—Lance, Paul and Kevin, have owned it. It has grown to ninety-seven employees with John Deere dealerships in four locations—Weslaco, Raymondville, Harlingen and Brownsville, and is one of the few major farm equipment dealerships in the Valley that is locally owned.

Barbee Neuhaus has earned its reputation as the premier supplier of farm and homeowner equipment for the Valley and northern Mexico with superior products and unequaled service. As agriculture in the Valley is changing with farmland decreasing and development booming, the firm is also changing to meet its customers' needs. As a service to its customers, the company sponsors owner-operator clinics in English and Spanish.

Diversifying from a concentration on agricultural equipment, the company now supplies some construction equipment and a complete line of lawn care equipment. Industrial customers select from reliable John Deere industrial scrapers and skid loaders. Homeowners and farmers have responded to the safety features, which are engineered into John Deere mowers, chainsaws, and hand-held tools.

Commercial managers of golf and turf also rely on Barbee Neuhaus products and services to handle challenges like football and soccer

fields. And for young future farmers and homeowners, they carry a full line of miniature tractors and other child-sized equipment.

Agricultural equipment at Barbee Neuhaus has become more fuel efficient, more environmentally friendly, highly computerized, and easier to operate. More complex equipment means more highly skilled service technicians. Field service trucks now have laptop computers equipped with diagnostic programs.

Earl Neuhaus and his sons believe in the slogan: "Still reliable, still John Deere, and serviced by the best."

Above: This Barbee Neuhaus John Deere dealership has been located on thirty-acres by Expressway 83 in Weslaco since 1976.

Below: From left, Earl Neuhaus and sons, Paul, Kevin, and Lance, own Barbee Neuhaus, which serves agricultural and commercial customers in South Texas and northern Mexico from four Valley locations.

SOUTH TEXAS INDEPENDENT SCHOOL DISTRICT

South Texas Independent School District (STISD) serves junior high and high school students throughout the Rio Grande Valley. Blanketing Cameron, Hidalgo and Willacy Counties, STISD overlaps twenty-eight other school districts, an area of 3,643 miles.

The only one of its kind in the state, the school district is comprised of four magnet schools:

- South Texas Academy of Medical Technology (Med Tech) in San Benito;
- South Texas Business, Education & Technology Academy (BETA) in Edinburg;
- South Texas High School for Health Professions (Med High) in Mercedes; and
- The Science Academy of South Texas (Sci Tech) in Mercedes.

Offering Valley students with an educational alternative, STISD schools provide a personal environment, a rigorous academic curriculum and hands-on training in the fields of education, business, technology, medicine, engineering, architecture and computer science. The mission of STISD is to nurture the development of lifelong learners as they excel in a challenging, focused curriculum that leads to successful post-secondary education and careers.

A public school district, STISD does not charge tuition and provides bus transportation to all of its students. Further, the schools maintain an open-enrollment policy, meaning any student with the desire to learn and work hard can attend as long as he or she resides within the tri-county area.

The Texas Education Agency and Southern Association of Colleges and Schools accredit all four schools. The schools also have partnerships with major universities, such as Baylor College of Medicine, Rice University, Rochester Institute of Technology and University of Texas at Austin. Over ninety-five percent of STISD graduates continue their education at major universities or technical colleges.

Created in 1964 by the Texas legislature, STISD first provided education to disabled youth who were then excluded from public education. It started as South Texas High School, a residential school in Edinburg. A few years later, STISD opened another school by the same name in Harlingen, which was relocated to San Benito in 1982.

In 1983, lawmakers extended STISD's purpose to permit the operation of vocational magnet schools. STISD pioneered public education by opening three new schools within a decade: Med High in 1984, Sci Tech in 1989 and The Teacher Academy of South Texas (Teacher Academy) in 1993.

In 2003, after adding business and technology programs, the Teacher Academy was renamed BETA. That same year, South Texas High School was redirected and became Med Tech.

Though the district's mission has evolved since 1964, STISD continues to provide educational and occupational training to students with special needs through the Half-Day Career & Technology Program offered at each school.

Valley Insurance Providers lives up to its acronym—VIP—by treating all customers as Very Important Persons, regardless of the type and size of the insurance policy. That philosophy has been associated with the independent insurance agency since its founding in 1939 as the San Juan Insurance Agency and its incorporation in 1977 as Valley Insurance Providers by then-owner Cruz Cantu.

Sheila Dunagan acquired Valley Insurance Providers in January 2003 coming full circle because years ago she was trained by her father in his local insurance agency. Dunagan's vision for her company positions Valley Insurance Providers as doing more than just selling insurance policies: it tailors insurance for the specific needs of the individual, family, vehicle, home or business. As an independent agency, VIP seeks the best coverage at the most affordable price thanks to its long-standing direct appointments with more than thirty insurance carriers and access to several more providers. By continually tracking changes in coverage and rates, VIP is able to provide the most suitable protection against the insurable risks for each customer.

Dunagan emphasizes VIP's service commitment, which is revealed in attention to details, big and small. VIP stays open during the lunch hour and on Saturday mornings to assist busy customers and even makes office and house calls. Located in Pharr, VIP concentrates on clients in the Upper Valley, although the staff serves customers scattered across Texas.

As president, Dunagan expanded the company's policy lines to include more traditional commercial coverage along with more personal lines to insure homes, health, life and autos. The company's commercial customers range from hotels and restaurants to banks and builders. These respected companies and their owners rely on VIP to secure the most cost-effective workman's compensation, professional liability, property, and bonding coverage.

Experienced agent Andy Alvarez specializes in payment and performance bonds for contractors. Whether the contractors are building outlet malls or executive homes, Alvarez counts on good working relationships with his clients and their insurers, which allow him to suit the coverage to the situation. A Valley native and PSJA graduate, Alvarez began working in an insurance agency while a student at Pan American University twenty-five years ago and found he was a natural for the field. He plans to continue playing an active role in the growth of VIP while assisting professionals in obtaining the special coverage they need.

Valley Insurance Providers is proud to assist its commercial and personal lines customers as they grow and prosper with the Rio Grande Valley. Visit the company's website at www.valleyinsuranceproviders.com.

VALLEY INSURANCE PROVIDERS

Below: Sheila Dunagan.

Bottom: Andy Alvarez.

RIO GRANDE VALLEY PARTNERSHIP

The Rio Grande Valley Partnership, with its prestigious, sixty-four year legacy of building progress and prosperity, exists to cultivate opportunities. A Chamber of Commerce for the whole Valley, the Partnership fosters the relationships and coordinates the programs that advance regional economic development.

Created in 1944, it unites a diverse and distinguished roster of leadership from across four counties to a common purpose: to improve how we live and how we earn a living in the Rio Grande Valley.

Currently guided by forty board members and buttressed by as many as 500 members, the Partnership pursues a vigorous not-for-profit program of work to benefit every single section of the Valley. Often the Partnership works quietly; always it labors modestly. Careful not to duplicate the efforts of local Chambers of Commerce, the Partnership complements their work from behind-the-scenes, anonymously galvanizing regional support.

Unapologetically, the Partnership is not a social club. The purpose of this organization is not simply "getting together;" rather, this organization is driven towards purpose by working together. Agile and available, the Partnership meets to task, like securing a private project or promoting a public issue.

For example, in 1994 the Partnership facilitated the Empowerment Zone application that resulted in one of only three rural awards in the nation, bringing a $40 million federal investment towards infrastructure and job development. Likewise, the Partnership facilitated three comprehensive Mobility Plans; the first two successfully secured $500 million in current projects and the most recent plan seeks $3.5 billion in improvements,

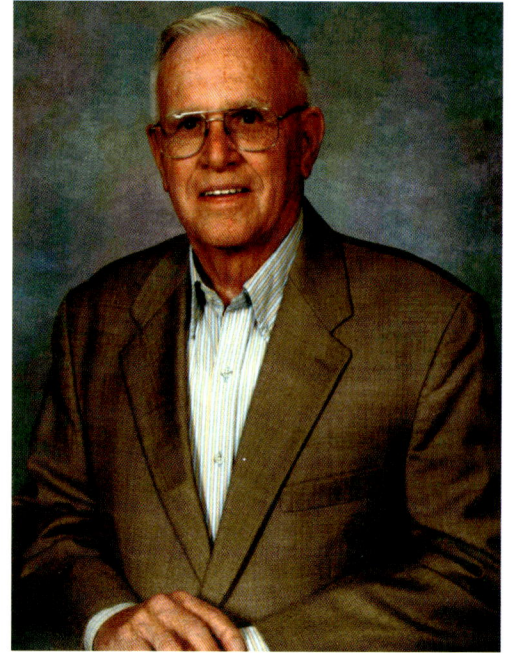

including a highway loop around the Valley to make commerce more efficient.

Remarkably, the Partnership is not a PAC. The Partnership does not represent any political party, nor does it contribute dollars towards any political agenda. Instead, the Partnership contributes to the discourse; as a ready resource, it equips decision-makers, public and private, with the information and contacts they need to successfully realize their objectives for the general good and advancement of the entire region.

Though the Partnership works closely with various government entities, it is not beholden to any of them. Unlike many local chambers and economic development councils, the Rio Grande Valley Partnership does not receive any public funds toward its operational expenses, relying solely on the continued support of Valley businesses.

For more than six decades, drawing on the convictions of its founders and the strength of its members, the Partnership has created a legacy of opportunities and accomplishments. We invite you to join that legacy, sharing in the fellowship of productive people who support regional initiatives as they seek an opportunity for themselves.

For additional information on the Rio Grande Valley Partnership, visit www.valleychamber.com on the Internet or call 956-968-3141.

The busiest airport in the Rio Grande Valley, McAllen-Miller International Airport handles over 60,000 aircraft arrivals and departures annually. Commercial airlines, private aircraft, and military planes choose McAllen as the destination of their domestic and international flights. Conveniently located in the city for maximum accessibility, the airport is ringed by quality hotels and restaurants and La Plaza Mall.

Four airlines connect McAllen and the Rio Grande Valley to anywhere in the United States or the world with one-stop service to the largest air travel hubs in the United States. Continental Airlines flies to Houston Intercontinental with onward connections to 290 destinations. American Airlines goes directly to Dallas-Fort Worth, and Delta Connection flies McAllen passengers nonstop to Atlanta, the nation's largest airport and Delta headquarters. From those major airports, destinations in the U.S., Europe, Asia, and Latin America are in easy reach.

From McAllen International, Allegiant Airlines flies directly to Las Vegas up to five days a week.

With the McAllen Metropolitan Statistical Area among the fastest growing regions in the U.S., the McAllen area now includes increasing numbers of young families with disposable income and a high interest in easy access to places like Disney World, Las Vegas, and tropical beaches. Attuned to passengers' preferences, McAllen Airport is catering to those customers by bringing in low-cost, direct destination or point-to-point carriers such as Allegiant Airlines.

Amid the bustle and gleam of contemporary air travel at McAllen International, the main lobby honors aviation's past with a 1910 White monoplane replica suspended overhead, a conversation piece that was built from plans published in *Popular Mechanics*.

For business travelers, the McAllen airport provides a complimentary business center with free wireless Internet connections and private desk spaces. Conference and meeting facilities in the airport terminal ease the strain for people who do business in multiple cities.

Those waiting for arriving passengers or for departing flights appreciate the airport's two cafes and bar. The UETA Duty-free store and gift shop serves not only international passengers but also stocks magazines, newspapers, gifts, and snacks for domestic passengers.

The airport's general aviation segment provides aircraft charters, air ambulance service, flight instruction and aircraft rentals.

MCALLEN-MILLER INTERNATIONAL AIRPORT

SAN BENITO CONSOLIDATED INDEPENDENT SCHOOL DISTRICT

Above: La Encantada Elementary kindergarten student Jonathan Braunstein was photographed during the school's graduation photo session. Pre-kindergarten and kindergarten students throughout the district "graduate" into their next year of academic succession. Throughout the next twelve years, these young learners will be offered progressive, innovative, and top-notch academic programs, a wide array of extracurricular activities, and state-of-the-art technology.

Below: Three-year-old Andreina Contreras is a participant in the San Benito CISD's "Building Bridges" program offered free of charge to eligible migrant families. Implemented through the local Migrant Education Program "Building Bridges" places an emphasis on early education enhancement and performance opportunities for the youngest migrant students.

San Benito's first city school opened in 1907, soon after the city was named, in recognition of the importance of educating the young. Now, 100 years later, with the population booming and a quality education important as never before, San Benito schools strive to have their students achieve educational equity and excellence through the collaborative efforts of 1,400 teachers, paraprofessionals, support staff and administrators. In a safe and secure learning environment, over 10,000 students in the SBCISD are receiving an education that prepares them to become lifelong learners. At the school district's seventeen campuses, students take advantage of outstanding academic programs and state-of-the-art technology as they learn the language, math, science and other skills that will enable them to succeed.

The community's support for San Benito's schools has been constant and overwhelming, as witnessed by three successive bond elections that have funded new school construction and building upgrades. Four new SBCISD facilities opened in 2006: Riverside Middle School, the Sonny Brazil Agriculture Science Complex, Judge Oscar De La Fuente Elementary, and Bobby Morrow Stadium. The progressive, innovative Veterans Memorial Academy offers in-depth learning in specialized fields of study, including health, law and research, fine arts and engineering that enable students to graduate with marketable skills.

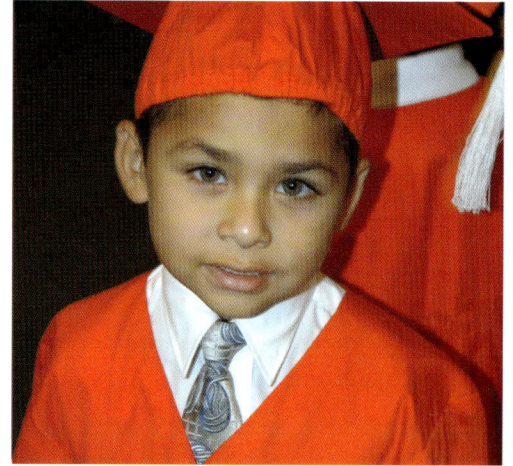

To ensure that the youngest students learn fundamental skills early, the district assigns most of its instructional aides to pre-kinder, kindergarten and first grade classrooms. Texas Reading First grants, totaling $1.5 million annually, reinforce the fundamentals so no child is left behind. Technology grants of more than $6 million in recent years have resulted in the integration of more than 4,500 multimedia, networked computers in the district. A 2007 goal is to have every eighth grade student technologically literate. Students from kindergarten to twelfth grade who have mastered computers are proud to showcase their digital and multimedia skills in the Annual District Multimedia Contest.

The school district is committed to addressing every student's unique requirements through diverse, dynamic programs for gifted and talented, migrant, special education, Bilingual/ESL, Career and Technology Education, advanced placement, and dual enrollment. The Parental Involvement Program empowers parents so that they, too, can help their children succeed. The award-winning KSBG-TV 17 offers quality educational programming.

Numerous activities, such as sports, music, UIL, and student organizations, engage students, enriching them mentally and physically. San Benito's After school programs range from the award-winning chess club and karate classes to tutorials. Thanks to a security force, which includes ten certified police officers, the safety of students and staff is well covered, allowing students to concentrate on learning.

KRGV NEWSCHANNEL 5

Breaking news, breaking stories, breaking the mold: KRGV NEWSCHANNEL 5 brings viewers the region's most important news stories, severe weather coverage and ABC's liveliest entertainment, both broadcast and via the Internet. Wherever the news breaks-anytime, anywhere-KRGV NEWSCHANNEL 5 anchors, reporters, producers, and technicians work hand in hand to get the information accurately and immediately to the public.

Established more than fifty years ago in Weslaco, KRGV NEWSCHANNEL 5 has taken the lead in broadcast technology on the air and on its popular website, www.newschannel5.tv. The First Warn 5 Storm Tracking Center is South Texas' best-equipped television weather center. Using Nexrad powerful Doppler Radar that can see inside and through storms as they approach the Valley in real time, along with Titan, the most powerful weather tracking system in television history, the First Warn 5 Storm Tracking team of meteorologists can pinpoint the time of impact, location and intensity of each storm.

KRGV NEWSCHANNEL 5 has been owned since 1964 by the Manship family corporation, which has overseen the continuous updating of broadcast equipment and a responsive approach to news coverage. Since 2003, the station has broadcast a digital, High-Definition signal that provides sharper images for viewers. KRGV NEWSCHANNEL 5's website offers expanded news coverage, adding depth to broadcast stories with unaired footage. Viewers can download free streaming videos of news, weather and selected network shows or check KRGV NEWSCHANNEL 5 archives to download podcasts and vodcasts of favorite episodes of ABC hit programming.

Reaching into the community, KRGV NEWSCHANNEL 5 demonstrates its commitment to the public interest through locally-produced, award-winning education programs, such as Masterminds, as well as in public service projects. "Wherever we see a need, we step in to help," explains Ray Alexander, longtime general manager. The station has organized the Valley Relief Fund to help victims of hurricanes, tsunamis and other natural disasters. They have rallied community support for multiple projects including Teach the Children, which provides clothes and school supplies for first graders. KRGV NEWSCHANNEL 5 is the Valley administrator of this project, and 100 percent of the donations go to purchasing the supplies and clothing. Tim's Coats is another long time project with over 60,000 coats donated to the Valley's needy to date.

Whether delivering up-to-the-minute news, tracking severe weather or helping those in need, KRGV NEWSCHANNEL 5 is an active part of the Rio Grande Valley community.

Rio Grande Valley Adult Geriatric

Dr. Pedro E. McDougal grew up in the Dominican Republic, a beautiful Latin American Island located in the Caribbean. The spirit and charm of the Dominican Republic is captured in its music, food, and national pastimes. Known for its professional winter baseball, handcrafted cigars, and annual music festivals, the culture of the Dominican Republic is never stodgy, or boring. It is always an artful and colorful expression of life. His parents actively involved in radio broadcasting as station owners and directors in the Dominican Republic. Dr. McDougal at the age of six, had his own children's radio program called The Kingdom of the Children, but despite the excitement of broadcasting, he decided to become a physician to help others.

In 1989, Dr. McDougal graduated from the Medical School of Pontificia Universidad Catolica Madre y Maestra in his hometown of Santiago, Dominican Republic. He completed his residency in Internal Medicine at the Cornell University-affiliated hospital St. Barnabas in The Bronx, New York in 1995. The same year, he became Board Certified in Internal Medicine, placing in the top ten percent nationwide.

Dr. McDougal started his private practice in South Texas in 1995. After ten years of establishing a very successful Internal Medicine practice in Weslaco, Texas, his interest in improving the care of senior citizens led him to a one year fellowship in Geriatric Medicine at University of Texas Health Science Center San Antonio (UTHSCSA) which he completed in 2005. Now Board Certified in Geriatrics, Hospice and Palliative Medicine.

Geriatrics is the medical specialty devoted to improving the health, functioning and well being of the elderly. As a geriatrician, Dr. McDougal recognizes the interdependency of medical, social, and psychological issues in the overall health of patients. Geriatrics is all about function and quality of life of the elderly. "We take care of older people, not just their diseases."

Palliative medicine focuses on the active total care of patients by managing pain and minimizing emotional, social, and spiritual problems at a time when a disease is not responsive to active treatment. Palliative care seeks to control suffering and to give patients the highest possible quality of life.

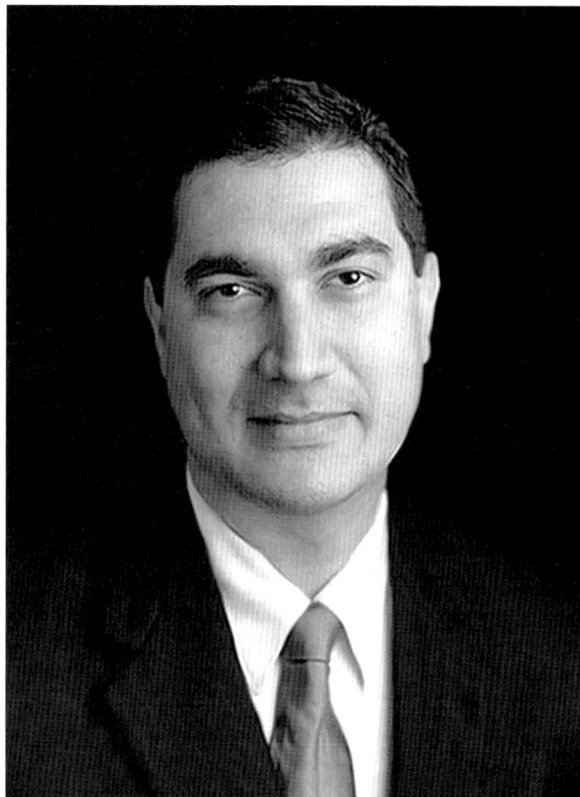

Dr. McDougal is committed to teaching physicians and other healthcare professionals how to provide optimal care for the elderly. He is chief of the Geriatric Division at UTHSCSA's Regional Academic Health Center where he is also a clinical associate professor in the Department of Medicine. Additionally, Dr. McDougal is the Clinical Instructor for Physician Assistant Studies Program at the University of Texas-Pan American and as invited faculty, has lectured Geriatric Fellows at UTHSCSA.

In 2006 in recognition of Dr. McDougal's academic achievements, community involvement, and medical leadership, the American College of Physicians elected Dr. McDougal a Fellow of the College, a stellar distinction.

Dr. McDougal and his wife Fifa, an interior designer, are the proud parents of Emmanuel, Grace, and Luis. The family loves to travel and spend quality time together.

The year 2007-2008 marks the twenty-fifth anniversary of Exquisita Tortillas. This once small locally owned tortilla manufacturing and distribution company in Edinburg, Texas has grown dramatically over the past quarter century. From its humble beginnings with three employees in a renovated old Valley Transit Bus Station to its most recently developed 70,000 square foot manufacturing facility with nearly 250 employees, President and Chief Executive Officer J. Humberto Rodriguez has been at the helm since day one.

The son of an Edinburg dry goods store owner, Rodriguez got his start in business working for the Azteca Milling Company. In the late 1970s he traveled throughout the United States selling corn flour mix that simplified the manufacturing process of tortillas. Then in 1983, he formulated his own vision to produce the finest and freshest tasting tortilla products, delivered fresh each and every day to his customers, which now number in the tens of thousands from the Rio Grande Valley to Laredo, Corpus Christi, San Antonio, Austin, El Paso, Del Rio and everywhere in between.

His secret throughout the years has been to consistently provide his customers the highest quality tortilla products made from the finest ingredients with a minimal use of preservatives. Although, Exquisita tortillas, for the most part, have a shorter shelf life (two to three days and up to three weeks refrigerated) than most of its competitors, the benefits are undeniable. A low preservative tortilla, simply tastes better and has the ability to be reheated several times over. And this is just what every Exquisita customer has come to expect and appreciate over the years...a better and fresher tasting tortilla, Just Like Mama makes!

Throughout the years, Rodriguez has managed to maintain and hold onto his company's market share by consistently delivering, on a daily basis, the highest quality tortilla products and by expanding his market base by adding new and diverse products throughout his company's sophisticated distribution network.

Today, the company distributes and sells a variety of food products including flour and corn tortillas, cheese sauce, tortilla chips, pork skins, tostadas, chalupa shells, hard taco shells, and Mexican sweet bread. Their newest product, a ready-to-cook flour tortilla has literally taken the market by storm. Second in line, is the traditional corn tortilla, which represents sixty to seventy percent of the market demand.

With tortillas generally considered the fastest growing bread product in the world today and a major food staple set to rival traditional white bread in the United States alone, the future continues to look bright for Exquisita Tortillas. Locally, in South Texas, this could not be truer. In fact, it would be impossible to imagine Mexican-American cuisine without tortillas and tortilla chips right alongside the traditional chicken or beef, beans and rice meals. For thousands of years, corn tortillas have been a staple of the Hispanic population since the Spanish Conquistadors first settled in South Texas and Northern Mexico. Rodriguez is banking on the fact that the popularity of tortilla products will not change...just grow stronger! As he often says with a smile, "Man cannot live by bread alone. So, eat plenty of tortillas!"

Above: Exquisita Tortillas are delivered fresh everyday from it's 70,000 square foot manufacturing facility to customers throughout the Rio Grande Valley, Corpus Christi, Laredo, San Antonio, Austin, El Paso, Del Rio and everywhere in between.

Below: J. Humberto Rodriguez, President and Chief Executive Officer, Exquisita Tortillas, Inc.

RODRIGUEZ, COLVIN, CHANEY & SAENZ, L.L.P.

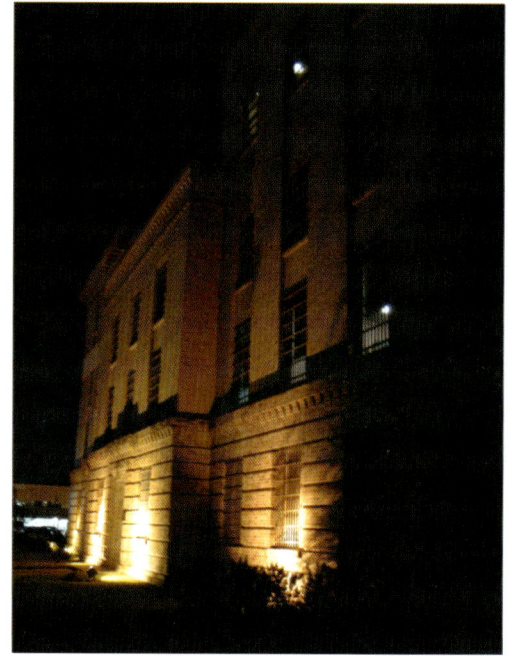

Above: The 1912 Cameron County Jail at night.

Below: The Hardy Memorial Conference Room at the Firm's offices.

The law firm now known as Rodriguez, Colvin, Chaney & Saenz, L.L.P., began in 1950, when the General Solicitor for the Missouri Pacific Railroad suggested to two Brownsville attorneys that a merger of their firms would better enable them to represent the Railroad. The firm of Sharpe, Cunningham & Garza was born and it began representing the Rio Grande Valley business community in civil litigation. Over the next decades, the firm continued to grow and emerged as a major South Texas law firm. During that time, founding partner Reynaldo G. Garza was appointed to the bench as the first Hispanic federal district court judge, and Cunningham and Sharpe parted ways. T. Gilbert Sharpe joined forces with another established Brownsville attorney, Benjamin Hardy. The firm of Hardy & Sharpe became the firm of Hardy, Sharpe & Rodriguez when University of Texas law graduate Eduardo Roberto Rodriguez made partner. In subsequent years, Norton A. Colvin, Mitchell C. Chaney, and Jaime A. Saenz became name partners. In 2004 the firm assumed its current name of Rodriguez, Colvin, Chaney & Saenz, L.L.P. Current senior partner Eduardo Roberto Rodriguez served as the president of the State Bar of Texas in the 2005-2006 year.

The headquarters of Rodriguez, Colvin, Chaney & Saenz, L.L.P. are located in the restored 1912 Cameron County Jail. The 1912 Old Cameron County Jail Building was

designed by renowned San Antonio architect Atlee B. Ayres and the original structure was completed in 1912. The fourth floor was added in approximately 1929 by Ayers and his son and partner Robert Ayers. It served as the county jail and sheriff's office from 1912 until 1978, when new facilities were completed. The building is of architectural importance due to its Classical Revival-style, a distinctive feature for this type of building. A one-story outbuilding dedicated to food service was erected in the back courtyard in the 1940s. From 1978 to 1992 the jail was unused. In 1992 the Jail Building was sold by sealed bid to "La Carcel, L.L.P."—a partnership consisting in large part of the named partners in Rodriguez, Colvin & Chaney, L.L.P., which completed its restoration in 1993. The building has been listed on the *National Register of Historic Places* by the United States Department of the Interior, is a recorded Texas Historic Landmark, and is found on the Brownsville Heritage Trail. Rodriguez, Colvin, Chaney & Saenz, L.L.P., remains committed to the preservation of Brownsville's heritage and to the civic life of the community. Rodriguez, Colvin, Chaney & Saenz, L.L.P., and its members are major supporters of Brownsville community institutions, and they serve in a variety of capacities at local schools, churches, and charities.

The City of Alamo's Mayor, Commissioners, Alamo Economic Development Corporation, and staff embarked on an ambitious plan six years ago to revitalize this community of 16,000. They shared a visionary approach designed to keep pace with the rapid growth of the Rio Grande Valley and the ever-increasing demand for public services. Because of Alamo's remarkable record of managing its finances, the city has been able to allocate $15 million for improving city streets and buildings, drainage, parks and utility infrastructure. The projects completed—a City Hall, the Public Library, and the Public Works Service Center—indicate the city's public service commitment. The former city hall has been transformed into a police station and the one-time library now houses the Municipal Court. In the design stages are a new fire station, a public safety substation, and a 500,000 gallon elevated water tower. The new thirty acre $2.2 million Sports Complex/Community Park is enhancing Alamo's quality of life as are frequent concerts in Central Park and monthly Market Day.

Sound fiscal management has enabled the city to keep its property tax rate at a low fifty-nine cents per $100 of valuation. The city collects approximately ninety-two percent of its current year tax. Alamo collects 99.5 percent of every monthly water, sewer and garbage bill, resulting in water and sewer rates that are among the lowest in the Valley.

Alamo's strong economic footing recently attracted a Wal-Mart Super Center, two motels, an 80,000 square foot medical center, and a 56,000 square foot retail complex along with several small retail businesses. The surge in sales tax in the last five years, from $1 million to $2.4 million, has played a major part in financing the city's makeover and has facilitated other economic development projects and federal grants of approximately $6.2 million.

On the site that 250 years ago was a Spanish land grant, known as Agosterdero del Alamo, for its abundant Alamos or cottonwood trees, the Alamo Townsite Company was formed in 1918. Today the city's economy has diversified from its agricultural origins to take advantage of its natural resources. Alamo is the Gateway to the Santa Ana National Wildlife Refuge, the region's most popular nature-watching destination with approximately four hundred species of birds, hundreds of butterfly species, and new treetop observation tower for spotting thousands of migrating hawks. The historic Alamo Land and Sugar Company headquarters has been restored as the Alamo Bed & Breakfast. Each winter Alamo's population doubles as Winter Texans return to their homes on the border. Alamo is the "Refuge to the Valley."

The dedication of Alamo's new Public Library marked another milestone in the city's ambitious revitalization plan.

HARLINGEN MEDICAL CENTER

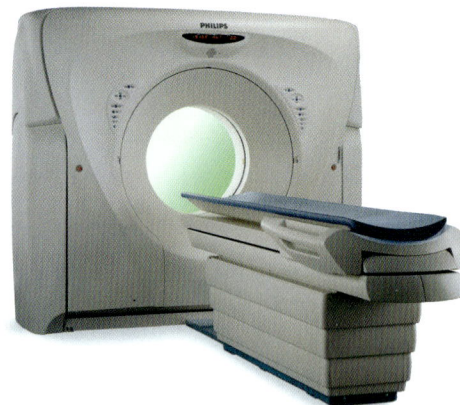

Above: A 64-Slice CT scanner.

Below: Harlingen Medical Center is located at 5501 South Expressway 77 in Harlingen.

Harlingen Medical Center is taking the lead in bringing high quality, accessible and compassionate healthcare to the Rio Grande Valley. The hospital is managed and staffed on the concept of patient-focused care, striving for better medical outcomes and more attention to the individual patient's needs and comfort.

Harlingen Medical Center's mission is to be the provider of choice for the medical, surgical, and diagnostic services it offers as well as a champion of health and wellness for the community. In the twenty-four-hour Emergency Room and in the operating rooms, from the dedicated staff in the Wound Healing Center to the orthopedist setting a child's broken arm, the hospital's skilled medical professionals apply state-of the-art technologies and advanced treatment options to ensure patients receive outstanding medical care.

The trained, caring staff at Harlingen Medical Center's twenty-four-hour Emergency Room knows the difference between an Emergency Room and a waiting room. Harlingen Medical Center pledges that a qualified medical staff member will see patients within fifteen minutes of completing registration.

Every patient room is private and designed and equipped for every stage of treatment, so patients experience less shifting from room to room. Cross-trained nursing teams provide consistency and continuity of care, reducing patients' stress. Patient services are decentralized and located close to patient rooms to reduce patient transport. Family members have round-the-clock access to the patient, and a sleeper bed is located in each room. The Women's Center addresses special needs from childbirth on with six home-like labor and delivery rooms, two OB/GYN operating suites, and a nurse to patient ratio that ensures close personal nursing care.

Ever-expanding ancillary services further demonstrate the hospital's commitment to comprehensive, accessible medical care. At Harlingen Medical Imaging Center, a full range world-class array of diagnostic imaging equipment provides precise images rapidly, enabling physicians to make accurate, timely diagnoses. The 64-Slice CT scanner can detect heart disease in the earliest stages with fast, non-invasive and painless scans. The Open MR creates images of internal organs and structures with greater detail than ever before with a comfortable, sideways entry couch and faster exam time to reduce patient discomfort. 4-D Ultrasound results in efficient, rapid assessments.

In the Wound Healing Center comprehensive wound care, including Hyperbaric Oxygen therapy and individualized treatment programs, focuses on difficult to heal wounds. The Sleep Center monitors patients' sleep patterns to diagnose the cause of excessive loud snoring, morning headaches and related symptoms to allow doctors to prescribe appropriate treatment.

At Harlingen Medical Center each patient is treated like family. For additional information on Harlingen Medical Center, visit www.harlingenmedicalcenter.com.

When Kent Shepard was working toward his marketing degree at Texas A&M University, he never dreamed that in just over two decades he would head his own successful insurance agency.

Nor could he have known that his deep interest in history and community service would lead him to be 2006 chairman of the board of the Museum of South Texas History. Another unexpected honor would come when he was elected 2007 Chairman of the Rio Grande Valley Partnership, a regional chamber of commerce promoting the interests and issues of businesses across the four counties of the Rio Grande Valley. He is also on the McAllen Rotary board.

Though quiet and unassuming, his leadership qualities come through in both business and community.

Kent's insurance career began in 1985. He gained broad experience in all lines of insurance before starting Shepard Insurance Agency in McAllen, Texas in 1998. The agency specializes in providing personalized insurance coverage that meets the needs of families and businesses.

He has gathered a strong staff of insurance professionals who offer quality quotes and plans for all personal and business insurance needs, including commercial bonds and professional liability.

Minnie Villareal brings forty-five years of experience in both personal and commercial lines to her post of marketing specialist for new commercial lines accounts at Shepard's. She says that, even with all of her years of experience, insurance is never boring and she learns something new each day.

Yolanda Alonso, commercial lines account manager, is a lifelong resident of the Rio Grande Valley who wants her customers to consider her their business partner and establish a strong and long-lasting relationship.

So does Betty Mendez, personal lines account manager, who says, "I find insurance to be an exciting and never-ending learning experience, and I take pride and joy in working with all of our agency clients." Other professionals on the staff also enjoy meeting the clients and providing excellent customer service.

The Shepard Insurance Agency is a proud founding member of the Alliance Group, LLP with the Smith Reagan Insurance Agency of San Benito. While each firm operates independently, through this marketing alliance they strive to bring exceptional services and insurance products to their clients in the Rio Grande Valley.

Shepard Insurance has extended its services with an online presence at www.shepins.com.

Above: Kent Shepard.

Below: The insurance professionals of the Shepard Insurance Agency of McAllen.

REGION ONE EDUCATION SERVICE CENTER

The Region One Education Service Center, along with the nineteen other education service centers across the state, was first created in 1965 when the 59th Texas Legislature authorized regional media centers. Education Service Centers were reauthorized in 1967 expanding their purpose to include the provision of educational services to school districts and the coordination of educational planning in the region. Again, in 1969, the role of the education service center was broadened to include participation in a statewide system of computer services, including provision of technical assistance. It was during this same time that the Texas legislature created the service center by dividing the state into twenty geographical regions. Even then, Region One area educators were already leading the way. The schools in this South Texas area had by this time pooled their resources together to form co-ops for media services, professional development, and curriculum development. It was this South Texas association that lobbied the legislature to approve a measure that would create the Education Service Centers. For this reason, the South Texas region was granted the distinction as Region One Education Service Center.

At this time, technical assistance may have involved providing film strips to schools, but today, the services of the Region One Education Service Center have expanded to include video conferences across continents, students traveling to our nation's capitol to experience leadership training, the integration of technology into classroom settings, the creation of business cooperatives to purchase anything from bus parts, electricity, food products to library materials, and the fusion of a community's culture into content core areas of the curriculum. There may have been changes along the way; however, the goals of the Region One Education Service Center—to provide quality services to school districts, to

positively impact student achievement, assist school districts in operating efficiently and effectively, and to provide support for the implementation of statewide initiatives—have never wavered.

Located in South Texas on the United States/Mexico border, Region One ESC serves over 373,000 students in the seven county areas of Cameron, Hidalgo, Jim Hogg, Starr, Webb, Willacy, and Zapata. The territory of the Region One Education Service Center was once considered one of the smallest of the twenty statewide service centers in terms of student population; today, however, Region One is considered a fast growth region and the fourth largest service center in the state, trailing Houston, Dallas, and Forth Worth. This year, Region One's student population surpassed that of the San Antonio area. Based on student populations over the past five academic school years, the student population is forecast to grow at a steady rate. Growth trends indicate that the Region One student population will exceed 400,000 students by 2008.

Prepared with this information, the staff of the Region One Education Service Center continues to focus its professional development offerings in the core content areas to improve overall academic performance. To further meet the individualized needs of the teachers, campus leaders, support personnel, and administrators, all initiatives and programs of the service center are intentionally developed with its clients, educators, and students in mind. The Region One Education Service Center is recognized statewide for its commitment to improving the education levels and economic vitality of its citizens and it will continue to implement educational initiatives via community and business partnerships to provide the best educational opportunities for students within the Region One service area.

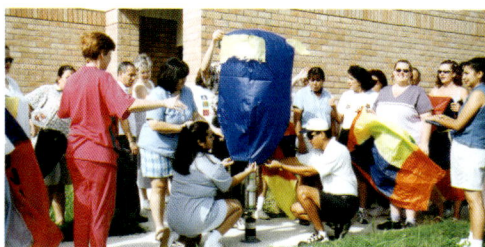

RAYMONDVILLE INDEPENDENT SCHOOL DISTRICT

At Raymondville Independent School District our mission is to deliver a superior academic and technological education so that 100 percent of our students graduate and become productive citizens with a strong sense of social and civic responsibility in a multicultural society while integrating the agricultural, historical, recreational, and cultural aspects of South Texas and northern Mexico that are unique to the Rio Grande Valley.

Raymondville Independent School District is the largest school district in Willacy County. The School District employs over 400 people. Raymondville I.S.D. proudly serves more than 2000 of the finest students in grades pre-kindergarten thru twelfth grade. Raymondville I.S.D. consists of four different campuses:

- The Raymondville High School was originally constructed in 1924. It is now a Historical Center and a Farm and Ranch Museum. This museum is located on South Business Seventy-Seven. A second high school was built in 1952, which is now known as the Old High School. In 2001 a new high school was built just east of the Old High School on FM Road 3168.

- The Myra Green Middle School was originally constructed in 1959 and named after the late Myra Green, a former long time teacher. On November 6, 2007, voters overwhelmingly approved a bond election to replace Myra Green Middle School with a new campus that is expected to be built by 2010. The proposed location for this campus is north of Burnett Stadium.

- The L.C. Smith Elementary was originally constructed in the 1950s and named after former teacher, coach and principal, the late Leighton "Pop" C. Smith. The campus was then demolished and reconstructed in 2000. The L.C. Smith campus is located on North First Street.

- The Pittman Elementary was originally constructed in the 1920s and named after the late Addie Pittman, a teacher and principal who worked for Raymondville I.S.D. for nineteen years (1926-1946). It was then demolished and reconstructed in 2001.

Raymondville I.S.D. is also the fiscal agent for Wil-Cam Pupil Services. The Wil-Cam CoOp provides Special Education services to six different school districts, which are Raymondville I.S.D., Lyford C.I.S.D., San Perlita I.S.D., Lasara I.S.D., Rio Hondo I.S.D., and Santa Rosa I.S.D. These entities comprise Raymondville I.S.D.

Top: Raymondville High School.

Left: L.C. Smith Elementary School.

Middle: Myra Green Middle School.

Bottom: Pittman Elementary School.

PALENQUE GRILL

Francisco "Pancho" Ochoa has always been a creator of new ideas like famous "Pollo Loco" restaurants that have been popular since its inception. The Ochoa Family was doing so well with Taco Palenque, that some of the other cuisine concepts were in the back burner. Just like Pollo Loco, Pancho Ochoa dreamed of a new concept of Mexican restaurant and created Palenque Grill.

The first Palenque Grill opened in 2005 in Laredo, Texas, just across from the Jockey Arena and in a few months, expansion of the building was necessary due to the success of the new concept. A few months later, Francisco, Jr., opened a second Palenque Grill in McAllen and to date both restaurants are very successful.

Palenque Grill has more variety in food as compared with their Taco Palenque restaurant chain and is known to have delicious seafood like Pescado Sarandeado, which is one of their specialties. Fajitas, Pollo Asado, and Carnitas de Puerco Michoacan style are some of the other popular signature entrees that Palenque Grill offers.

Aside from those dishes, they offer Costillas Asadas, Ribeye, and Albondigas de Camaron. The Ochoa family manages their restaurants with impeccable service. They constantly train employees to make sure that customers are satisfied and leave happy. The Ochoa family is also known because they are in partnership with the community. They participate by giving back as much as they can to the communities where they do business.

It is important to say that the Ochoa family who came from Sinaloa, Mexico decided to set up shop in South Texas because they consider this to be a fertile area for business and full of opportunities. Francisco Ochoa, Jr., considers his father Pancho, Sr., to be a unique creator and leader of the family. The Ochoa family has also created hundreds of jobs and opportunities for many South Texas residents.

Pancho Ochoa and his family come from humble beginnings but through dedication and a great passion to serve have become icons of South Texas. To learn more about Palenque Grill and the Ochoa family, visit www.palenquegrill.com.

Sponsors

About the Narrative

Eileen Mattei

Freelance writer Eileen Mattei writes travel and nature articles that appear regularly in *Texas Highways* and *Texas Parks and Wildlife* magazines. A love of travel, the outdoors, and telling a good story led her to writing, following her first career in aquaculture.

Her business articles and ghost-written columns have been published in the Rio Grande Valley for the last twelve years, and she recently helped update a major Texas travel guide. She lives in Harlingen with her husband Guy.

About the Photography

Rebecca Rivera

While studying art and graphic design at the University of Texas-San Antonio, Rebecca Rivera discovered her calling: photography. She returned to her native Rio Grande Valley after studying with noted photographers.

A member of the Texas Professional Photographers Association and the Professional Photographers of America, Rebecca Rivera specializes in contemporary and artistic portraits. She is best known for her distinctive wedding photographs that capture the moment.

"I feel blessed to document lives, events, and places, creating photographs that will be treasured by generations to come," she says from her studio in Mission. She is pursuing the designation of Certified Professional Photographer. Her photography has been exhibited by the Rio Grande Valley Art Guild.

Rebecca Rivera lives in Mission with her husband, son, and daughter.

For more information about the following publications or about publishing your own book, please call
Historical Publishing Network at 800-749-9790 or visit www.lammertinc.com.

Black Gold: The Story of Texas Oil & Gas

Historic Abilene: An Illustrated History

Historic Albuquerque: An Illustrated History

Historic Amarillo: An Illustrated History

Historic Anchorage: An Illustrated History

Historic Austin: An Illustrated History

Historic Baldwin County: A Bicentennial History

Historic Baton Rouge: An Illustrated History

Historic Beaufort County: An Illustrated History

Historic Beaumont: An Illustrated History

Historic Bexar County: An Illustrated History

Historic Brazoria County: An Illustrated History

Historic Charlotte:
An Illustrated History of Charlotte and Mecklenburg County

Historic Cheyenne: A History of the Magic City

Historic Comal County: An Illustrated History

Historic Corpus Christi: An Illustrated History

Historic Denton County: An Illustrated History

Historic Edmond: An Illustrated History

Historic El Paso: An Illustrated History

Historic Erie County: An Illustrated History

Historic Fairbanks: An Illustrated History

Historic Gainesville & Hall County: An Illustrated History

Historic Gregg County: An Illustrated History

Historic Hampton Roads: Where America Began

Historic Hancock County: An Illustrated History

Historic Henry County: An Illustrated History

Historic Houston: An Illustrated History

Historic Illinois: An Illustrated History

Historic Kern County:
An Illustrated History of Bakersfield and Kern County

Historic Lafayette:
An Illustrated History of Lafayette & Lafayette Parish

Historic Laredo:
An Illustrated History of Laredo & Webb County

Historic Louisiana: An Illustrated History

Historic Midland: An Illustrated History

Historic Montgomery County:
An Illustrated History of Montgomery County, Texas

Historic Ocala: The Story of Ocala & Marion County

Historic Oklahoma: An Illustrated History

Historic Oklahoma County: An Illustrated History

Historic Omaha:
An Illustrated History of Omaha and Douglas County

Historic Ouachita Parish: An Illustrated History

Historic Paris and Lamar County: An Illustrated History

Historic Pasadena: An Illustrated History

Historic Passaic County: An Illustrated History

Historic Philadelphia: An Illustrated History

Historic Prescott:
An Illustrated History of Prescott & Yavapai County

Historic Richardson: An Illustrated History

Historic Rio Grande Valley: An Illustrated History

Historic Scottsdale: A Life from the Land

Historic Shreveport-Bossier:
An Illustrated History of Shreveport & Bossier City

Historic South Carolina: An Illustrated History

Historic Smith County: An Illustrated History

Historic Texas: An Illustrated History

Historic Victoria: An Illustrated History

Historic Tulsa: An Illustrated History

Historic Williamson County: An Illustrated History

Historic Wilmington & The Lower Cape Fear:
An Illustrated History

Iron, Wood & Water: An Illustrated History of Lake Oswego

Miami's Historic Neighborhoods: A History of Community

Old Orange County Courthouse: A Centennial History

Plano: An Illustrated Chronicle

The New Frontier:
A Contemporary History of Fort Worth & Tarrant County

The San Gabriel Valley: A 21st Century Portrait

The Spirit of Collin County